My One and Only Piece of Hand Luggage

Gareth P Jones

Grosvenor House
Publishing Limited

All rights reserved
Copyright © Gareth P Jones, 2024

The right of Gareth P Jones to be identified as the author of this
work has been asserted in accordance with Section 78
of the Copyright, Designs and Patents Act 1988

The book cover is copyright to Gareth P Jones

This book is published by
Grosvenor House Publishing Ltd
Link House
140 The Broadway, Tolworth, Surrey, KT6 7HT.
www.grosvenorhousepublishing.co.uk

This book is sold subject to the conditions that it shall not, by way of
trade or otherwise, be lent, resold, hired out or otherwise circulated
without the author's or publisher's prior consent in any form of
binding or cover other than that in which it is published and
without a similar condition including this condition being
imposed on the subsequent purchaser.

A CIP record for this book
is available from the British Library

ISBN 978-1-80381-762-0
eBook ISBN 978-1-80381-763-7

Dedicated to my wonderful wife, Sue.

Contents

Acknowledgements	vii
Introduction: Memories on a Bike	1
Through the Land of Song – 2008	9
D-Day Thoughts – 2009	18
Downhill All The Way – 2010	37
Turn Left at Dunkirk – 2011	57
No Later Than 1957 – 2012	75
Down Under – 2013	94
A Pilgrim's Trail – 2014	108
The Second Prettiest Chunk – 2014	127
Enter the Red Dragon – 2015	142
Iceland Delivery – 2016	160
Looking for a Scottish Moose – 2017	175
The Bear Essentials – 2018	192
'Oh yes, sir – most Definitely' – 2019	216
The Craic – 2023	243

Acknowledgements

I would like to thank my wife, Sue, for making my efforts into something understandable.

My daughters Ceri, Nia and Ami and their husbands Tom, Richie and Andrew for their full support, especially when they have had to endure my incessant witterings about my adventures.

To Ceri for designing the book cover.

To my friend Clive, who gave me the confidence to travel abroad.

To Alan, who gave me the inspiration to cycle the world.

To my fantastic mother, extended family and friends who continually ask me, 'How's the cycling going?'

For Julie and the team at Grosvenor House Publishing Ltd for all their hard work.

Finally to all those nameless people who helped me reach my destination.

Pencil drawings by author.

Introduction
Memories on a Bike

Pentre-Willey

My earliest memories was in the late 50s as a three-year-old living in a semi-detached farmworker's house close to the market town of Welshpool. Those distant memories – twin-seated wooden outside toilets, pumping water from the garden, watching rats scurrying around the henhouse, walking with Mum over the bridge to Welshpool, and seeing horseracing for the first time on next door's small television – remain just as vivid today.

I can still remember the time when, as a four-year-old, I sat on the seat of what I can only assume was a large lorry, waving our house goodbye for the last time. It was an exciting time for us, because we were moving 21km away to a small Montgomeryshire hill farm, with the strange sounding address of Pentre-Willey. Now, as you can imagine, it wasn't a name that you would readily tell anyone, especially your peers, and throughout my childhood it took a lot of coaxing before I would grudgingly divulge it to anyone. Fleetingly, I thought that all my prayers had been answered when Dad said that he had been looking at a farm to buy, but my bubble was quickly burst when he told me that it had the equally embarrassing name of The Cock Shutt.

Despite the embarrassment of having such a strange address, its origins have always intrigued me and a few years ago I took the time to visit the National Library of Wales in Aberystwyth to research it. I was shown maps of the area but frustratingly it only showed our little garden, which, for some reason, is on the other side of our lane. The helpful library staff suggested that seeing as we were close to the Shropshire border, I should study the library archives in the county town of Shrewsbury. Frustratingly, on arrival, I discovered there were no records there either. Mind you, the staff was equally helpful by suggesting that I visit the National Library of Wales in Aberystwyth to further my search…!

Meanwhile, I asked many native Welsh speakers if they could shine some light on this enigmatic name. It was suggested that it could be someone's name, e.g. Gwilliam's village. Another suggestion was that it had a connection with the Old English "welig" (willow) and "lēah" (woodland clearing, glade). Another was that it was Pentre ewyllys – the will village. My own theory is that it could have been a place where a willeying machine was used to open up or pull wool fibres apart. Who knows?

Despite Dad's efforts of periodically trying to buy a larger farm, it was never to be. I think in hindsight it was a good thing for them, because they spent 34 happy years there, creating a very happy childhood for me, my older brother, Philip, and younger sister, Margaret.

My formative years living on this small farm instilled in me a love of the countryside – not necessarily of farming, but an appreciation of all the good things that come with living on a farm, e.g. animals (domestic and wild), the ever-changing seasons which the farm revolved around, a sense of responsibility, plus a good work ethic, which always pleased Dad.

Having said all that, our farm was quite remote. Yet, I'm sure that it hadn't always been the case. No doubt, in the past, our lane, which continued on past the farm and out across the hill, had been a well-used artery – most probably used by drovers leading their stock to the markets over the border into England. Now, sadly, that busy artery terminates a little way past the farm at a derelict cottage, with mature trees and brambles securely barring the way and thus making further progress impossible. As a consequence, you never saw anyone popping in, or people passing by. If anyone came, then they came to see you. This meant that outside of school we had little interaction with kids of our own age. But, as those years passed, stronger bonds developed with others of my age. Unfortunately this would mean travelling to meet them and as my parents were hard-working, very much tied to the farm, I felt that it would be pointless asking them to start transporting me around the area to see my friends. So, an independent mode of transport was needed.

Now, this was easier said than done. As the name implies, you don't get a hill farm on flat terrain. It is either straight up or straight down, which proved the case at Pentre-Willey. It is situated halfway up, but thankfully under the snowline of the famous 24km-long Kerry Ridgeway (Ffordd Las Ceri). This ancient trade route stretches east from the Cider House Farm, near the village of Kerry in Powys, to the market town of Bishop's Castle in Shropshire, and is more or less the border between Powys and Shropshire. At 1000 feet above sea level, the ridgeway conjures up stunning views of the beautiful hills and valleys of Mid Wales on one side, and the Shropshire Hills on the other. If you were lucky, from certain points along the ridgeway, the majestic mountains of Snowdonia (Eryri) could just be made out on a clear day. I'm certain that you would have to travel a long way to better such a view of Mid and North Wales.

On the farm, we were just as lucky with the view we had. As well as the ridgeway sweeping majestically up behind us, we had the commanding Corndon Hill sitting directly in front of us, with the distant denim blue hue of the Berwyn Mountains in the far distance to admire. However, with all these stunning views comes a caveat. The wind (usually cold) was always blowing down between the house and the farm buildings, quickly taking the shine off any prolonged view-watching and making us sometimes wish that we lived down on the wide flat valley below. Knowing there was always a steep hill to climb up or down; the thought of cycling slowly along narrow, flat meandering country lanes was always a distant dream. Yet, despite these drawbacks, I still craved a bike – I needed a bike.

At that time, the only push bike available on the farm had no saddle or tyres. Where this bike came from, I had no idea, but it was available to me to learn how to ride across the yard by placing my right foot on the left pedal in a type of a side saddle manner in order for me to gain my balance and some confidence. Cycling down the yard was never considered, because like the saddle and tyres, the brakes were non-existent and the thought of careering headlong into the mixen (manure heap) didn't fill me with much joy.

After gaining a modicum of confidence going across the yard, I then pestered my parents to buy me my first proper bike. A bike was soon spotted in the advertisements page in our local newspaper and because my father wasn't able to take me to see it, it was left to my mother to take me one evening to view it. Now, this new-looking bike was presented to us both in the back of a dark and dingy farm building. The owner of the bike assured us that the bike was of the highest quality and it would in fact last for years. Nevertheless, the way that his two sons were sniggering behind him should have sounded alarm bells ringing in our ears, but I was so determined that this was in fact the bike of my dreams, Mother had no choice but to buy this outstanding metal steed for me.

Alas, in the cold light of the following morning, the excitement of showing off our new purchase to my father was soon to be tempered by his somewhat negative comments. To be blunt, he asked us why we had bought such a poor specimen of a bike. It was only then, when I realised that what I thought were shinny chrome wheels, were in fact rusty wheels sprayed with aluminium paint and both tyres were flat, plus the brakes didn't work either. But at least it did have a saddle.

Knowing I had to make the best of a bad purchase, I fixed those minor issues and used the bike to travel up and down those steep roads surrounding our farm until a bigger bike was found. This new bike was a black Hercules, which I decorated with wrappings of black and white chequered *GO FASTER* insulation tape. It was in a better condition than my first bike, with better brakes, which came in handy when going down the infamous Pullets Bank – although a well-placed foot scraping along the high ditches helped to decrease the speed when the brakes occasionally gave out. This black, single speed, sit-up-and-beg style bike suited me well enough and it allowed me, at the age of 15, to cycle the 5km to either catch the service bus to take me the 16km to work in Newtown, or to have a lift with a work colleague in his brand new minivan, or occasionally with a neighbour.

Whether I caught any of those modes of transport to work all depended on whether I had suffered a puncture on the overgrown 0.5km lane from our farm to the road. Annoyingly, our lane had sharp stones imbedded in it, just ready to prey on a soft, poorly pumped-up tyre, so it was inevitable that punctures were a constant threat. Even trying to cycle on the grass-covered middle part did little to prevent that scourge of cycling, because it harboured all kinds of thorns and small sharp branches, just waiting for an unsuspecting tyre. My father, the forever pragmatist, would at these times suggest that I should start out earlier and push the bike along the lane. As you can imagine, this never happened, I just hoped for the best and continued mending punctures whenever they appeared. Mind you, cycling on tarmac roads didn't always guarantee a puncture-free existence either. At certain times of the year, hedge trimmers would leave a mat of small lethal branches strewn across the road, again just waiting for you to ride over them – a bit like cycling across an Indian bed of nails.

Cycling in the wintertime proved to be no walk in the park and it certainly provided more than my share of butt-clenching moments. My daily descend on an icy or snow-covered Pullets Bank required nerves of steel. Luckily, the rough unkempt sides of the road provided just enough grip to make my way gingerly down and, as mentioned before, a well-placed foot scraping the high ditches also proved an efficient method of slowing my speed down. I'm sure, these days, that level of commitment to put life and limb to the test during such inclement weather in order to catch a lift to work would be a rare sight. Regardless of these annoying occurrences, my bike was a well-used mode of transport until, at the age of 17, I passed my driving test. With my newly discovered street-cred, plus Dad's beat-up green Morris 1000 van, my trusty bike was discarded and forgotten – never to be seen again.

The next 35 years saw me working hard as a carpenter/joiner, with weekends renovating our first home, and then building our own bungalow while raising our three lovely daughters with my wonderful wife, Sue. It was only then, after joining the local college of further education as a lecturer, teaching my love of carpentry, did I discovered that I now had a fairly sedentary lifestyle and would need to improve my overall health and fitness. So, I bought a second-hand Gary Fisher mountain bike.

Now, this was a shock to my fragile system, so I took it slowly from the start, cycling approximately four miles on warm sunny evenings after work. But when the evenings started to draw in, I felt it was too dangerous and too cold to cycle in the dark, therefore, I put aside a Sunday morning to get my cycling fix and it's amazing how quickly you develop a craving for this weekly dose of adrenalin and found myself cancelling everything that had been arranged in order to achieve this.

Don't get me wrong, I have a wonderful home life and feel very contented, but, like so many other men of my age, there is a small part of us that craves for a little bit of freedom and adventure before we feel it's too late. So, after increasing my Sunday mileage to around 50km, I started to not so much get bored with the same format, but I started to think of other routes and areas I could cycle through. A work colleague of mine had sown a seed by cycling in various countries. So, with that thought in mind, the distant hope of eventually cycling in other countries began to emerge. So I decided to look further afield.

However, to temper this burgeoning enthusiasm, I had to think about family and work commitments. I was certainly in no position to take a gap year off and travel the world with a load of sponsors in tow; therefore, I could only plan for a short adventure. After looking at maps of the UK, it was obvious to me that my first trip would be in Wales and what better first long-distance trip could I start with than the 322km National Cycle route 8 (Lôn Las Cymru) from Holyhead on the island of Anglesey, to our capital city, Cardiff.

I do not promise you a fun filled trip of a lifetime, or exotic reminisces, but it is an opportunity to experience what a person can achieve on a bike, with only a limited amount of time and money squeezed into a narrow window of anticipation. Why not come with me. You'll have a free ticket to ride and look at my world of cycling from over my shoulder – you can, if you want, give me free advice and council without the fear of reply or reprisal.

Now, slap on the udder cream, don your Lycra and we'll experience it all together.

Ffwrdd â ni (Off we go).

Through the land of song – 2008

Caernarfon Castle

While my initial thoughts of completing my first long-distance cycling trip were positive, I couldn't help but feel a certain amount of anxiety leading up to it. No doubt for proper cyclists, this relatively short distance would be more or less just a training exercise for them, to get their bodies into good shape, a distance familiar to them on a weekly basis. But for me, it was a whole new ball game, a big test of my physical and mental strength. There was no certainty that I even possessed any of the requirements needed to successfully complete this 322km unsupported trip. To me, this trip was a pedal rotation into the unknown.

Yet, through all of this uncertainty, a part of me kept saying that I was worrying too much. I knew that my bike was in good condition and well maintained. So, apart from the usual punctures, there shouldn't be any fears in that department.

Also, there were many suggestions and good advice from people who had ridden bikes (as well as advice from people who hadn't), so I listened gracefully to all of them, allowing them their council. But, in reality, it would inevitably be left to me to choose the best options.

The local bike shop gave me the best advice for most things, stating that good, well-padded cycling shorts were a must-have item (whether a middle aged man in Lycra is a sight to behold, remains a point of discussion). They also suggested that a spare tyre, inner tubes, puncture repair kits, plus an array of small tools and spanners should also be on my list.

Although I would be cycling in some beautifully remote areas of Wales, you are never too far away from small local shops and cafes, so, apart from the odd snack bar secreted on my person, I knew I wouldn't need to stock up with food for the day. However, securing accommodation for each night would mean me having to book ahead and I thought that this would put too much extra pressure on me to complete a certain daily mileage. So, I decided to carry a small one-man tent. This would enable me to either use one of the numerous campsites en route, or, as a last resort, I could go off-grid and find a quiet place to illegally wild camp.

However, with the addition of a tent come other items that I would need, e.g. sleeping bag, ground mat, hammer, etc. These would have to be the smallest and lightest I could source in order to keep the weight down to a bare minimum. Luckily, these extra items were easily found and together with casual clothing and wet weather gear stuffed unceremoniously into my two panniers, I was ready to go.

The eagerly awaited day finally arrived and after checking everything one last time, my wife, Sue, and our close friend, Liz, jumped into the car with me and we began the 2.5 hour journey up to the beautiful windswept island of Anglesey and its port of Holyhead (Sue would then drive the car back home).

I was confident that I had everything that I would need, but when we were approaching our destination, I realised that I had stupidly forgotten a very important item – my helmet! So, after waving Sue and Liz off, I turned my back on the number of cars making their way to the ferry port and sought out an outlet selling helmets. Luckily, a famous retail store was close by, where I bought the cheapest helmet available and with it securely strapped onto my head and facing south, my adventure began.

Cycling on the old A5 was a joy, with the road being only used by local traffic. The majority of the traffic I could hear was bombing along the A55 North Wales expressway. With adrenalin coursing through my body, it only took me an hour to re-cross the ancient island and reach the outskirts of Bangor, where I turned right on to the National Cycle route 8 and headed for the royal town and port of Caernarfon.

For 13km of this road, I had, over my right shoulder, a fantastic view of the 25km narrow stretch of the Menai Straits, which separates the island of Anglesey from the mainland. These vistas certainly took my mind off my now protesting leg muscles.

It was with much relief when I cycled slowly past the impressive 14th century castle constructed by order of King Edward I and entered the main square in Caernarfon. There, I chose a small café where I had to put my far from perfect command of the Welsh language to good use. The waitress seemed to understand me, so I felt good as I tucked into a very tasty prawn salad.

My choice of destination for the first day was Porthmadog, a beautiful Welsh coastal town 88km away from Holyhead. Luckily, the cycle path from Caernarfon ran at times parallel to the main road and I made good progress on the road and sometimes on the path. I was conscious of the fact that cycling on a main road is not always as safe as you would like it to be, so I thought it prudent to take a small detour up and away from the main road. Unfortunately, my decision didn't take into account my increasing weariness and the pull up the side of the mountain was a real effort on my now protesting body.

Needless to say, I eventually arrived fatigued in the beautiful town of Porthmadog. After enquiring at the local information centre, I found a beautiful campsite half a mile out of the town. Now, because my backside resembled the Japanese national flag, I decided to walk the half mile back into town, thinking I would find a cosy pub to relax in before finding a suitable restaurant for my evening meal, but I have to admit that I wasn't feeling too good, so I went to a small café and slowly drank a pot of tea. After 30 minutes I felt better and went to a pub for a drink and then to a fine restaurant. On my return to the campsite, I relaxed in their spacious bar and then repaired to my tent, a tired but contented man.

Now, one thing I didn't envisage before setting out on this mid-life quest was the length of time it took to dismantle my small tent and pack everything neatly into my panniers. It took a lot of discipline on my part to take my time in order for everything to be placed correctly, instead of just throwing everything in willy-nilly and hoping that the pannier flaps would fasten. It's amazing how frustrating this seemingly pointless exercise is when you're eager to get going.

The next stage would be a 96km journey to the small market town of Llanidloes, which would see me climbing over a part of the Cambrian mountain range at Dylife. I knew that this would test my overall fitness and determination, but naively

I thought that – seeing I had a good bike, with low gearing – I would be able to overcome the obstacle without any major problems.

Before testing myself on that mountain, I still had to follow the National Cycle route 8 running through stunning vistas and wooded valleys. However, if you religiously follow the cycle route, it can sometimes take you off the beaten track, and this happened when I approached the nuclear power station at Trawsfynydd. The route instructed me to take an overgrown, rarely used cycle path that skirted around the back of the station. This not only raises the risk of punctures; the foliage also wants to hold on to you at every opportunity. After eventually emerging bedraggled from this jungle, I vowed to keep to the main road from now on, and this new plan now rewarded me with a leisurely, mainly downhill ride into the market town of Dolgellau.

After a quick pit stop, I climbed out of the valley, en route to Machynlleth. While on this road, you cannot help but be in awe of the impressive Cader Idris which dominates the whole of the view on the right hand side of the road. While this ancient mountain solidly lying in the southern end of the Snowdonia (Eryri) National Park gives everyone who sees it inspiration, it doesn't give you any more strength while cycling, and it is at this point where I hit the wall (or bonked, in cycling terms). It was my own fault for not keeping hydrated enough during the morning. Having run out of water, I approached a roadside restaurant to ask for a glass of water. It was obvious at this point, that the landlady was not too impressed with the pathetic figure presented in front of her and promptly refused to let me darken her reception, but was gracious enough to give me a glass of water, which she insisted that I drank outside (maybe she had a bad experience with a middle-aged man in Lycra in the past – who knows?). Anyway, suitable rehydrated, I continued on to Machynlleth, where I stopped for a tasty lunch.

From this point on, I knew that the road over the mountain to Dylife would be a big challenge for me. Cycling 48km on a leisurely Sunday morning is one thing, but to be confronted with a 14km uphill section after cycling 64km is quite a different matter. But with no alternative, I took a big breath, selected my lowest gear, put my head down and slowly started the 1614ft ascent. After climbing for 10km, my energy was spent, so I took the only option open to me and that was to resort to walking for a while, then cycling where I could in order to reach the summit.

Despite a heaving chest, the effort was worth it because the views looking back towards the Snowdonia (Eryri) mountain ranges took what little breath I had away. I'm sure you would have to travel a long way to better such a view.

Now, in my mind's eye, the remaining 19km should be fairly flat, then downhill into Llanidloes – which was true while passing the old abandoned lead mines of Dylife – but, in reality, there were still two very steep hills that need to be negotiated before the longed for descent into the town and I have to admit that I could only walk those parts, because by now I was running on empty. This was despite what I hoped were shouts of encouragement from a car full of local lads.

Eventually my efforts were rewarded as I coasted into Llanidloes. On the outskirts, I found a campsite and after pitching the tent and freshening up, I walked (albeit slowly) into town for a meal. By now my throat was so sore from the exertions of climbing the hills, I asked for a cooling prawn cocktail in one of the pubs. It was so cooling, I quickly ordered another and, for my dessert, I downed a couple of glasses of equally soothing brandy before heading back to the campsite to fall quickly asleep.

The following morning, in the middle of the town, I spotted my brother, Philip, leaning on his shovel while watching his colleague digging a hole for a council sign they were erecting. He maintained that he had been working hard, but I had my suspicions.

I felt surprisingly good at the start of my third day, which saw me heading a further 80km south towards the county town of Brecon. Following the steep-sided valley from Llangurig to Rhayader, I again took to the cycle route 8, which followed the old road running parallel across the valley from the main road. After Rhayader, I found myself again stupidly following a dirt track up through the woods, well away from civilization, until I finally emerged in Newbridge-on-Wye and vowed for my own sanity that from now on, I would keep to the main road as much as possible.

Arriving in Builth Wells, I toyed with the idea of cycling on the B4320 over the hill and on to Brecon, but my dwindling enthusiasm for steep hills compelled me to continue on the main road down the stunning Wye valley to Llyswen. I didn't regret it for one moment. The fast flowing Wye River, famous for its kayaking and canoeing was a perfect partner to accompany me on my first adventure.

I found a beautiful campsite on the outskirts of Brecon, with a table flat pitch to erect my tent. After an evening meal, I settled down for the night, or so I thought. Young revellers returning from their evenings excursions had other thoughts. They kept me and the rest of the assembled campers wide awake into the early hours with their squeals of laughter and the sound of high-heeled shoes clonking up and down the metalled paths leading to their tents.

When I left the following morning, there was not a sound coming from them, no doubt having a well-earned rest. I thought about making appropriately loud noises to give them a taste of their own medicine, but I just quietly cycled away.

From Brecon, I could have taken the A470 straight to Cardiff, but due to the heavy traffic, I decided to take the back road to Merthyr Tydfil. It's a beautiful road, skirting around two reservoirs and then climbing up around the base of Pen y fan, the highest peak in South Wales. At 886m this mountain may not be the tallest, but with its wild open moorland, it's certainly a severe challenge for even the strongest and fittest soldier and is frequently used by the world-famous SAS as part of their selection process.

Arriving at Merthyr Tydfil, I joined the Taff Trail, which follows the course of the River Taff and uses old disused railway lines, canal routes and trails, so you can't really get lost. It was a pleasurable experience slowly making my way to my final destination in Cardiff. After stopping for lunch in the small village of Tongwynlais, I then headed to the Cardiff Bay waterfront.

On that final day, I had arranged for Sue to meet up with me at 5pm in Llandaff's Tesco shopping centre, so to make that deadline, I turned my back on the busy waterfront and quickly cycled up to the city centre, across Sofia Gardens and on to the quiet residential suburb of Llandaff.

With my watch proudly beeping 5pm, and a spring in my step, I bounded two at a time up the escalator to the café area and there, with a huge smug grin on my face, I walked up to Sue sitting at a table. It wasn't quite the romantic scene of us both flinging arms around each other as soon as our eyes met. It was more succinct, with Sue promptly telling me to turn around and take the car keys and put some decent clothing on. So much for hugs and kisses!

Thoughts in the car

I was buzzing on the 158km return journey. I wanted to tell Sue everything about my trip, every little detail (apparently, I have an annoying knack for relaying seemingly pointless information in minute detail). Fair play to Sue, it took a long time before her eyes glazed over with my pedantic account of the trip. But I felt so chuffed that I had successfully cycled diagonally across my beautiful Wales – with no apparent damage to me or the bike.

I know it was only a relatively short journey with some proper cyclists probably laughing out loud at my endeavour, but I knew that this was the start of a quest to cycle in other countries – and I couldn't wait.

Wales is my home. It has everything you need, from stunning views, ancient history, sublime food, with culture and language all thrown in. Next time you are thinking about going abroad, think again. Wales is much closer and you will be a guaranteed a fantastic time.

D-Day Thoughts – 2009

American Cemetery – St Laurent

After my initial successful cycling trip in Wales, I felt I had the world at my feet. I had enough experience of driving abroad and felt confident in my ability to deal with everyday situations. Driving abroad really makes you experience what those countries could offer. It forces you to confront your inadequate command of their languages, customs and driving regulations. It hardens you for the inevitable ups and downs, which always gives you such memorable experiences.

I know that many people who go on holiday would have worked hard all year and just want to get on any mode of transport and arrive at a resort and park themselves down on the side of a swimming pool and just relax for the duration of their holiday. This type of holiday doesn't really appeal to me and I find that I always have to challenge myself and do what other people might think is a stupidly hard way to enjoy a holiday.

I have to admit that our first holiday abroad hadn't been plain sailing. When we decided in 1997 to go with our friends, the Williams, to France for the first time, it was not only my first time abroad, but it would be my first experience of driving on the other side of the road. Our two families had a wonderful time, but as for the driving, it was a very nerve-racking experience, with me trying desperately to remember to hug the right hand side of the road at all times.

I have to thank my more experienced friend, Clive, who had been driving on the continent for many years for allowing me to hang on to his shirt tails (in reality, his back bumpers) when we made that relatively short journey from Cherbourg to Grandville. At the time, the distance of 105km seemed a lot longer and the sight of my white knuckles gripping the steering wheel lived long in my memory.

Reassuringly, with more holidays in France came more experience and confidence in my own ability to drive abroad.

I know the odd word in French and have a stock of half a dozen phrases, the first one being "beer s'il vous plait" and "la même chose", which means "beer please" and "same again". These two can get me through most situations. There are others that relate to car and travel issues, which thankfully I didn't have to use too often. So, when I analysed the most suitable country for my first foreign cycle ride, it could only be France. I like France. It's a beautiful country and if you make an effort with the language, then they will readily help you.

The next question I asked myself was, which area of France should I cycle in? Like most people, I have only a limited amount of time to devote to my cycling passion. This is approximately seven to ten days. So, a ferry from Dover to Calais, then a journey of approximately 525km along the Normandy coast line to Cherbourg seemed plausible to me. With a return ferry journey from there to Poole and a train journey home, I felt comfortable with this well-rounded trip.

When the early morning arrived for my first foreign cycle trip, I have to admit that I was feeling a little apprehensive standing on the platform at Newtown station. To tell you the truth, I hadn't even travelled on many trains and wasn't really sure of the protocols for ticket collection. Do I present my tickets at the ticket office before boarding or on arrival at a station? This must seem very odd to many people, but if you don't know, then you don't know, however simple it turned out to be.

With these doubts and my reservation tickets for my brand new Giant Defy bike and myself stuffed in my back pocket, together with my fully laden panniers, tent and accessories, I boarded the train en route to Dover. I knew I had to change at Galton Bridge-Birmingham to arrive at Marylebone station, and then it would be a relatively short cycle ride across London to Charing Cross station to catch the train to Dover.

Arriving at Shrewsbury station, I couldn't help but notice and hear the large amount of people who were noisily boarding the train at this point. I was mildly annoyed with them for this sudden intrusion into my quiet contemplation of my first foreign trip. Is this the norm, do all train passengers behave in such a manner? It wasn't until reaching Galton Bridge and then seeing some old school friends waiting with me for the connecting train to Marylebone when the penny finally dropped. Apparently, Shrewsbury Town FC was playing at Wembley stadium against Gillingham FC in the football League 2 playoffs.

So, after catching up on careers, loves found, loves lost and near escapes, we eventually approached Wembley and the imposing Wembley arch. The air of anticipation was palpable. A nervous, eager energy surrounded everyone wearing the club's blue colours. Excitement, good spirits, all wrapped with brimming confidence engulfed them as they spilled out onto the platform. I wished them all the luck in the world as the noise of their reverberating chants faded as the train quickly pulled away from the platform.

Cycling around London is not for the fainthearted, but to me it seemed quite straight forward. Maybe luck favours the stupid. Anyway, it didn't take me long to negotiate the 4km from Marylebone to Charing Cross, where I was greeted by the equally raucous and slow moving mass of Gillingham supporters exiting the station. I'm sure their celebrations were even louder on the return journey; because they went on to beat Shrewsbury 1-0.

While waiting for departure, it was announced that the two train carriages would split before arriving at Dover and for everyone to make sure that they are in the correct carriage for their continued journey. I really didn't know if I was in the correct one, or not, or if I was facing forwards or backwards. Would the train drive out forwards or reverse out? You would think that it would be very easy to have your destination displayed electronically in your carriage before starting out. Later, when the train approached the point where it divides, on-board announcements told me that I was in the correct carriage for Dover.

On arrival at Dover station, I needed to use the toilet. I was aware that I had a brand new bike with two fully-laden panniers. What should I do? Should I leave them unattended, or take them into the toilet block? I certainly drew quite a few stares of disbelief from fellow users when they saw me trying to keep the automatic door from closing with one foot while trying to push a fully laden bike through it. At least it prevented my possessions being stolen.

As many travellers crossing from UK to the continent will agree, sometimes you have to go through customs and sometimes not. So, as I cycled slowly from passport control, I was directed to go into the large customs building. As well as looking and feeling very small and insignificant in a building that caters for huge juggernauts, I must have also looked a little shady, which obviously warranted a rummage through my one and only piece of hand luggage. Disappointed or not, the officer soon let me through and on to the check-in desk.

Like many people crossing the channel, I have arrived and departed from Calais on numerous occasions. It's very popular and consequently, very busy. It certainly lives up to the title of the gateway to France. But, this time, instead of keeping left and following the majority of traffic using the N216 as they headed for the junction and the A16 AutoRoute, I turned right and headed for the town centre.

While planning my trip, I had printed out maps of the roads, towns, cities and campsites, which I thought may come in useful. I knew I had to find the D940 coastal road leading to Boulogne-Sur-Mer and my first campsite. After consulting my first map, it didn't take me long to find this road and I was soon happily on my way. I feel far more comfortable when I'm on a bike. You have time to assess any given situation and I feel that I'm in full control of my destiny. Apart from severe bike malfunction, I can deal with most situations which could befall me.

This air of confidence abated somewhat when I entered the commune of Sangatte. This area is synonymous with the refugee camp there, which was opened in 1999 by the French

Red Cross. It accommodated thousands of would-be asylum seekers attempting to travel to the United Kingdom. Desperate Middle Eastern and Asian families paid unscrupulous people-traffickers loads of money just for them in turn to exploit their dreams of a better life in the UK. Although the camp is now closed, I couldn't help but feel relieved that I was not in that same situation. I'm certainly aware and pleased to be living in a stable country and not be someone so desperate as to sacrifice everything that you know and hold dear. To have no choice but to escape your country of birth with only the bare essentials and travel thousands of kilometres to seek a better life for you and your family in a foreign country – it doesn't bear thinking about. And to cap it all, at the end of this arduous journey, being forced to live in a refugee camp in cramped and squalid conditions. What a choice, what an uncertain future!

A mixture of light showers and the clinging sea mist, accentuated the feeling of hopelessness as I tried to cycle as quickly as I could past this notorious camp, fearful that if I slowed down, the air of bad luck surrounding this area may have time to hop on-board and keep me company. Luckily for me, I was able to cycle off this feeling of desperation as I continued on the 45km stretch along the beautifully undulating coastal road.

It was early evening when I approached the outskirts of the ancient city of Boulogne-Sur-Mer. Luckily, the D940 continued along the harbour and into the city. I knew I had to take the first bridge on the right over the River Liane and up a small hill leading to my campsite in Le Portel. In my research, I had highlighted campsites with either a bar or restaurant, which would save me looking for them further afield. So, when I approached reception at the Camping Le Phare d'Opale, I was delighted to see a group of people inside its bar enjoying a glass of wine.

I checked in and was instructed to continue on past the static caravans and up on to an adjoining sloping field overlooking the Strait of Dover (Pas de Calais). There, I could pitch my tent anywhere that caught my fancy. Seeing there were no demarcations of pitches, I chose a flattish spot halfway up the field. Why I chose a pitch halfway up the field and not closer to the bar, I couldn't tell you, but after securing the tent I made my way back down to enquire at reception about much needed sustenance. However, on arrival, I was greeted with a statement that the bar was closed and they didn't serve food. To say I was disappointed would be an understatement. I had been travelling since early morning and it was now 7pm and I just wanted to sit down, relax and have some food and drink.

In order to appease the gods of hunger, the only option for me was to walk into the centre of Le Portel and hope I could find somewhere to eat. However, my thirst was far stronger than my appetite; therefore, my first port of call was a bar. There was a restaurant close by, but because it's difficult to pack suitable clothing for a restaurant, and seeing as I was only dressed in jeans and a T-shirt, I didn't think that they would readily invite me into their bosom. So I just had another drink and some bar snacks to tide me over.

Just when I was starting to feel relaxed and relieved that I have made it this far without any problems, the barman indicated that the bar shut at 8pm. At this point, I gave him my most pathetically pleading look and persuaded him to give me just one more quick drink before I made my way back to the campsite.

As I walked back up the sloping field to my tent, I was greeted with a stunning sunset over the tranquil calm sea and I thought to myself, *what a perfect ending to a long day*. I soon fell into a peaceful slumber, no doubt snoring like a wounded warthog. However, around midnight, I woke up to uncontrolled shivering. The reason being that, in order to keep the weight down, everything I had to carry had to be as light as possible. Therefore, I only used the thinnest of materials, e.g. a sleeping bag liner instead of a proper sleeping bag, and a thin ground mat. Consequently, as the temperature dropped, these materials proved sorely inadequate. To overcome this discomfort, I covered myself with every piece of available clothing and huddled under my wet weather jacket and eventually returned to being a warthog.

The following morning began cool and clear and after striking camp, I again found the D940. This time it would lead me the 105km to the small fishing port of Le Tréport.

Within a few kilometres, I was cycling through gently undulating wide open fields and long straight roads. What a fantastic introduction to my first full day cycling in France. I was content and happily sucking in the beautiful vistas with every breath I took. I skirted around the fishing and leisure port of Étaples before swinging right over the yacht-filled estuary. The rest of the day was filled with hot sunshine, good roads and stunning scenery. I couldn't help but feel pleased with my choice of country. Given the luxury of time, I would have loved to have stopped in many of the small villages and ancient towns, which are popular with locals and tourists alike, but I had to be focused on making the required daily distances in order to successfully complete my journey.

By late afternoon I had arrived at Le Tréport. Camping Les Boucaniers was easy to find and a vast improvement on the previous campsite at Le Portel. The pitches were snooker table flat with grass baizes to match. It also boasted a licenced mobile catering facility. I was in heaven. This is exactly what I envisaged cycling in France would be.

After having a quick snooze in my lovely warm tent, I walked the short distance to the harbour, carefully peering down at the water several metres below. I had plenty of time to promenade and immerse myself in the atmosphere of the main street situated alongside the harbour. To reward this fantastic day, I had a leisurely glass of wine in one of the numerous café bars available.

On my return to the campsite, I tucked into a tasty meal of steak and frites, all cooked by a man of many talents. Our conversations revealed that he had lived in Manchester for a short time and therefore had a fairly good command of the English language. He was also the "go-to" man for anything and everything. He cooked the food, cut the grass, delivered the croissants and baguettes in the morning and maintained the site as necessary – a very handy man to have around the place.

The following morning began overcast with a threat of rain hanging in the air. I quickly struck camp and went to reception to check out. Unfortunately, it didn't open until 09:30 and as I waited, the half-expected sound of raindrops started splashing on the reception roof. As I cycled off down the road, the handyman stuck his head out from his bread van and showed another talent by singing, at the top of his voice, 'I'm singing in the rain, just singing in the rain.'

After a long slow pull up from Le Tréport on the 98km route to Yport, I called in at a convenient supermarché to buy sandwiches and water for breakfast and lunch.

Within two hours I had covered the 31km to France's first ever seaside resort of Dieppe. It is a very popular port, with ferry crossings from Newhaven, which ensures that Dieppe is a much-appreciated first port of call for UK people using the ferry to visit Northern France. Approaching the centre, I was well aware that this was the first big town on my trip. I must have been concentrating too much on my surroundings, rather than the road conditions, because, before I could avoid it, I must have caught my front wheel in some kind of old tram line. This made me immediately lose my balance and force me to attempt a less than dignified half-stumbling, half-running dismount in order for me not to come crashing down in the middle of the road. I must have looked quite shaken up, because one driver stopped to see if I was OK, which was very decent of him. After cycling along a tranquil tree lined boulevard, I turned left up a long straight and steep road out of the port.

The next 59km saw me cycling through more wide open productive farmland. Picturesque medieval villages came and went before I picked up a slow puncture. You can deal with a slow puncture easy enough. I just had to stop every 5km to re-inflate it.

I was nearing my destination of Yport, with only the port of Fécamp to be negotiated. Apparently Fécamp was a former home of the dukes of Normandy and more recently a major fishing port. Today, like so many coastal towns, it is very popular with tourists seeking out its rich history.

Like many small fishing villages, Yport is situated off the main road, nestling in the bottom of a narrow valley. The small road snaked its way down through beautiful deciduous woods, and levelled out into a tightly packed village, where most of the houses were built of red bricks and flint panels.

My campsite was situated in an elevated position beyond the village. To get there, I had to cycle past some attractive-looking restaurants and made a mental note of their position for a meal later that evening. Like the road into Yport, the road out snaked its way back up and out of the valley and as a consequence, I arrived at Camping Le Rivage huffing and puffing from the exertion of cycling up from the village. The weather had been OK, but the campsite itself had been subjected to heavy rain the previous day. Therefore, I had to choose carefully where I erected my tent.

After pitching on the driest part of a wet field, I enquired at reception about the quickest way back down to the village and which restaurant would he recommend. Frustratingly, his reply was not what I wanted to hear. He informed me that it would be pointless returning because, by the time I reached the village, all the restaurants would be closed. Sympathetically, he did offer to sell me a bottle of cider, a packet of crisps and a banana from his own supply. How could I refuse? I returned to my tent and tucked into my feast. Later, I repaired my slow puncture as the rain started to gently fall.

The next morning was horrible. Heavy drizzle and low sea mist were my only companions as I struck camp. This leg of my journey would be one of the longest, with a total of 116km.

Keeping to the small country roads, I re-joined the D940 at the small coastal town of Étretat, where I took advantage of the warmth of a small convenience store while stocking up for the day. This road took me to the major seaport of Le Havre and luckily it kept hugging the beach until it turned towards the docks. It was a little intimidating trying to weave your way in and out of the large industrial zone which was linked directly to the port. It was not obvious if the road I was on was the road out of this dock area.

Some of you might think, why didn't I avoid the docks completely, but then it would mean I would have to find a route through the maze of streets in the city centre. It would take a far more detailed plan of the city than the very basic map I had printed out, for me to successfully plot a course through it. Breathing a sigh of relief, I eventually found myself leaving the dock area. From there, I knew that I had to head for the only bridge that crossed the Seine estuary. This meant that I had to use the road which the large lorries and containers used to access the docks. Luckily for me, there was an excellent cycle path running alongside it and before long, I could see the formidable structure of the Pont de Normandie in the distance. Arriving at the bridge tollbooth, I was advised to be careful crossing the road expansion joint on the far side. They told me that, because my tyres were narrow, they could easily get wedged in the teeth-like joint and cause me to fall. I thanked them for their advice.

Now, anyone who has cycled over a large exposed bridge will tell you that it isn't just a case of cycling over it. There is a long gradual approach before you see the muddy water beneath you. It takes a long time and a lot of energy to cross it, especially when you are trying to fight against the wind pushing you from the direction of the river and the effect of the turbulence created by the speed of large vehicles pushing you the opposite direction. Eventually, I freewheeled down the other side and kept my eyes tightly closed as I crossed the expansion joint and onto the slip road to the old picturesque town of Honfleur.

This historic port has been painted many times by famous French painters, e.g. Eugène Boudin and Claude Monet, and I could see why. With slate-covered frontages, tree-lined streets and attractive harbour; I wish I had the time to sit down with paints and easel and just slowly sink into the canvas.

With another 54km to Ouistreham still to cover, I reluctantly left Honfleur and took the coast-hugging D513 to Trouville-sur-Mer. This was another popular seaside resort for the impressionist painters and their memorable scenes of the promenading 19th century bourgeoisie. The popular and romantic town of Cabourg came and went and, as I headed for

Ouistreham, I was worried that I was becoming a little too blasé, failing to appreciate the beautiful countryside and well-kept towns and villages of this stunning Normandy coastline.

On arrival, I soon located my campsite and, as normal, discovered that at this time of the year, the camp facilities were not available to me. So, in order to find something to eat, I went for a walk. Unfortunately, I was again unsuccessful. I'm sure if I had chosen to use my bicycle instead of walking, I may have found somewhere open further away, but the thought of getting back on my bicycle and searching for a restaurant on the off chance it may be still open didn't fill me with a lot of enthusiasm. With no chance of tucking into a tasty meal, I was left with little choice but to return to my tent and slowly eat my last banana and drink my last bottle of water.

Lying in my tent, feeling a little sorry for myself, my thoughts of discomfort soon evaporated with the realisation that within 300m of my campsite lay the beach (code name Sword) which was the eastern flank of the five main landing areas for the Allied invasion of German-occupied France in June 1944. My slight discomfort was nothing compared with the conditions that would have to be endured by those brave soldiers and local civilians alike. The horror they must have experienced and witnessed doesn't bear thinking about. And as I lay there, knowing there was a high probability that the remnants of that June battle lay cold and quiet beneath me, suddenly, my banana and water tasted all the sweeter.

The next day saw me cycling the whole length of the Normandy coastline from Sword beach at Ouistreham to the Western Utah beach 103km away. It wasn't long before I arrived at Arromanches (code name Gold), where the British forces had started an early naval bombardment and a subsequent amphibious landing. As a family, we had visited this village on our first trip to France and I was well aware of the Mulberry harbour which had been towed over from Britain and erected just off the beach to assist the Allied forces unloading their supplies. To emphasise this recent history, there is a particularly poignant and well-presented war museum by the harbour, with thought-provoking videos to watch.

If you are thinking of visiting this area of France, then you must visit the American Cemetery and Memorial, which is situated close to the village of Colleville-sur-Mer overlooking Omaha Beach. For our family, this was a beautiful place and a humbling experience. As soon as we entered it, the sheer scale of the cemetery took our breath away. What started out as a noisy day quickly became a quiet thoughtful journey. Looking along the hundreds of headstones, we marvelled at the symmetry, which from every direction were all in perfect alignment. We all felt that this attention to detail was a fitting monument and an example of the respect given for the ultimate sacrifices which all heroes make. But today, on my own, I just sat outside a small café in quiet contemplation.

Leaving my thoughts behind, I continued making my way around the headland and passed Grandcamp-Maisy, where an overgrown German heavy artillery battery was discovered. It is now a museum with over 4km of original German trenches, bunkers and buildings.

To continue towards the final D-Day landing beach (code name Utah), I had to cut south to the narrow end of the Canal de Carentan à la Mer and the town of Carentan-les-Marais. From there, the D974 took me north, after which I then branched off on the D913 and headed for Utah beach.

Approximately 6km from the beach is the small village of Sainte-Marie-du-Mont. In June 1944 it was occupied by

60 enemy soldiers. This ideal location was chosen by the Germans as they used the church tower as an observation post. They found that on a clear day it provided them with an unobstructed field of vision all the way to the sea. To counteract this, American paratroopers were dropped in the dark and were given the responsibility for clearing a route for thousands of soldiers arriving by sea from England. After fierce fighting around the village and area towards the beach, the area was secured, making Sainte-Marie-du-Mont the first community to be liberated.

After passing through this historic village, I soon arrived at Camping Utah Beach, wet and cold from the heavy drizzle which had accompanied me for most of the day. There, I was pleasantly surprised to see that they had a bar and shop. So, after erecting my tent, I went to buy some food. At this time of the day, there was little choice of food available, however from a rather empty looking shelf, a tin of tuna and some bread caught my eye. Standing at the counter, I must have looked very wet, cold and miserable, because the lady who served me kindly offered to warm the tuna up. I secretly hoped that she would also provide me with a plate and utensils, but no such luck. Pathetically, I returned to my wet tent and sat cross-legged and used my fingers as utensils to prise out the hot tuna.

During the afternoon, I had noticed a large number of American service vehicles driving around the area. I learned subsequently that it was the 65th anniversary of the D-Day landings in Normandy. Later, in the bar I could only assume that some of the people seated were either ex-US service members, or their families, engaging in quiet conversation, along with their own thoughts.

Returning to my tent amongst the sand dunes and hollows, I suddenly realised that the topography of the campsite was most probably not a result of natural forces, but carved out by intense warfare, 65 years ago. Again, I was very conscience of the fact that I had been born after such a horrific time in history and as a consequence, spared the horrors of living or fighting through it.

The penultimate day rose clear and free from the heavy drizzle of the previous day. I had a spring in my step and was looking forward to cycling this last full day. At 54km, my route up the east coast of the Cherbourg peninsular was relatively short, so I took my time, appreciating the good weather and quiet roads.

I stopped in the pretty town of Quettehou to buy my daily quota of bananas and then decided to stop at the fishing port of Barfleur for lunch. I chose a lovely restaurant opposite the harbour. After a week on the road, I was very aware that I was not looking at my best. With no facilities to keep my cycling clothes clean, I would have not been surprised if, looking at my dishevelled state, the proprietor of a harbour restaurant refused me entry. Yet, surprisingly, he didn't. Maybe it was because at this time of the day the restaurant was unusually quiet, but he graciously invited me in with open arms. I love fish, so tucked into a delicious salmon salad, all washed down with a small glass of beer.

My last campsite was at Camping Anse du Brick. It is situated 12km from Cherbourg and is on an elevated piece of land overlooking the rugged coastline. As I approached reception, I noticed a large sign for a pizza parlour beyond the building. I thought, *what a perfect place to spend my last night*. It had lovely flat pitches surrounded by privet hedges, which I used to dry out my damp clothes. I draped everything, including the tent, on top of them as the hot sun beat down. Within 20 minutes everything was tinder dry. I went back to reception and asked when the pizza parlour would be open. To my utter dismay, the lady told me that it didn't open on Thursdays. On hearing this unwanted statement, it would have been very easy for me to buy a bottle of wine from the well-stocked shelf behind her and drown my sorrows, but I chose not to. She did, however, inform me that there was a lovely restaurant just at the entrance to the site and it would be open at 6pm.

After walking along the stony beach for an hour, I went back to my tent and tried to find the least crumpled T-shirt and made my way the 200 metres back down to the entrance and walked into the restaurant. Seeing that it had only just opened, I was the only customer there. I perused the menu and hopefully chose a fish dish and a glass of white wine to complement it. When it came, it was very tasty and I thought to myself that this was a far better option than eating a pizza back at the site (I don't really like pizzas anyway). Sitting at a table which overlooked the small bay, I couldn't help but think that this was a very pleasant way to end my last full day in France.

I really should have known better, my smugness was quickly wiped off my face with the arrival of a migraine. Although I don't suffer as much as some people do, never the less, it can be quite nasty. I thought to myself, *what shall I do now?* The strong headache pills I take to lessen the severity can help a little, but I quickly decided that another glass of wine would either kill or cure, so I had another two just to be certain. I then made my way back to the tent and fell into a painful sleep.

The next morning I rose with a somewhat tender head (of course from the migraine and not the wine), and promised myself that I would resist the urge to head a football, if one ever came flying in my general direction. Within an hour I was on the road to Cherbourg and three hours later relaxing in the lounge on the ferry sailing over to the Dorset port of Poole.

From the port, I located Poole train station and settled down to a long day travelling back to Mid Wales. I had reserved tickets for myself for this return journey, but was conscious of the fact that my bike could be vulnerable out of my sight. Therefore, I gave up my seat to stand close to it in the area between carriages. The train was very busy at the time and I wasn't the only one using this space. About six squaddies were on leave and were enjoying a few tins of beer and as the journey progressed so did their enjoyment increase. At one time a male vicar came on board and had to endure an hour of friendly well-chosen expletives from them. I spoke to him later and he ensured me that he didn't mind being called "bish" and their crudeness was only words to be taken lightly.

Thoughts on the train

I was very pleased with my accomplishment and more than happy with my choice of country. Things that could have gone wrong didn't, e.g. cancelled trains, delayed ferry crossings, severe weather and mechanical failure.

I was disappointed with the lack of camp facilities. I had researched the route and chosen campsites which had advertised a bar/restaurant. However, to my dismay, I discovered that that didn't necessarily guarantee that they would be open and, if they were, they had closed early, compared to bars/restaurants in the UK.

I think I was a little naïve to think that every campsite would be fully open at this time of the year. My vision of warm sunny days and sultry nights relaxing at a superb restaurant, all clamouring for my attention, fell far short of that mark. It turned out that I was wet more than I was dry, cold more than

I was warm, hungry more than I was full, and thirsty more than I was quenched.

All said and done, I thoroughly enjoyed this first foreign cycling holiday. It gave me confidence and showed that I could deal with most situations that could arise – a real learning curve.

No doubt, most Brits have been to France, but this north Normandy coastline has a thought-provoking history to it and as a consequence ticks many a box. So, if you're into your history, then it's just a short hop to immerse yourself fully in it.

Downhill All The Way – 2010

John O'Groats

I believe that to truly call yourself a cyclist, then you should successfully complete a recognised route. The route that I have always considered a real challenge is the iconic End to End, LEJOG, or JOGLE. Whichever way you want to put it, if you cycle diagonally from northeast Scotland to southwest England, or the other way round, I think you can justifiably call yourself a cyclist.

All my life, I have admired the countless number of people who have, over many years, successfully completed this challenge. It seemed to me that it was a challenge only capable of completion by super fit athletes, people far better and stronger than I would ever be – an achievement only destined for someone else. I had heard that these super humans had completed this task on many different modes of human-powered transport. They include:

penny farthings, unicycles, conventional bicycles, tricycles, tandems, recumbent, wheelchairs and everything in between. They've walked it, run it, skateboarded it; hit a golf ball all the way there. Someone has even swum it. What can I say? If I could just complete it on a conventional bicycle, then I would be a very happy member of this group of people.

To make this trip worthwhile, I decided to use this opportunity to raise funds for the local Air Ambulance. Living in such a rural area, it is a must to have a fast and efficient method of transporting an ill or injured person quickly to the nearest hospital.

Initially, I did think that I would need the help of a support team to successfully complete the trip, but after thinking about it, I felt it wouldn't be fair to ask close friends, or family, to take time off to help me in this venture. Therefore, I decided to take on this challenge unsupported and hope for the best.

Apparently, there are many routes you can take. As the crow flies, it is 970km. The more conventional routes are approximately 1400km. I just wanted to cycle the route as quickly as I could. The directional aspect of it, I decided, would be from John O'Groats to Lands' End, because I reckoned that, towards the end of the trip, there would be more accommodation available in Cornwall than in northern Scotland. But the main reason was that it's downhill all the way.

I researched the best route and the daily distances I hoped I could achieve. I had decided that I wouldn't need any camping equipment, because I hoped that I could secure accommodation en route. So, after filling my panniers with what I deemed was suitable, I set off once again from Newtown railway station on a long 15-hour journey up to Thurso, the northernmost town on the British mainland.

While John O'Groats is traditionally acknowledged as being the farthest diagonally from Lands' End, I chose Thurso as my first destination. This was the closest station to Dunnet Head, which is the most northerly point on the British mainland, and visiting it would satisfy my need to tick off a couple of boxes on my trip.

The train journey north was fairly uneventful, but a big thumbs up to Wigan station, which was bedecked with many hanging baskets and tubs of beautiful flowers. These made the approach to their station very pleasing to the eye. This cannot be said of the many other stations which I passed through.

Eventually I arrived at Waverley station in Edinburgh. From there my journey took me over the spectacular Forth bridge and up through the Highlands to Inverness.

Arriving at Inverness station was alarming and a little confusing. To start with, a station guard was telling some cyclists that they couldn't take their bikes on the train to Thurso. Also, there seemed to be two trains leaving at slightly different times going to Thurso. I just wanted to make sure that I was on at least one of them, so I took the first train, but that only took me as far as the small town of Dingwall. Frustratingly, I had to leave the train there and wait for the second train, which would then take me all the way to Thurso.

After looping inland from Tain to Lairg, the single-track line hugged the Moray Firth coastline, passing through many of the places I would cycle through on my way back down. Being so close to the coast afforded me fantastic views of grey seals bobbing in the surf and oyster catchers on the beach.

At Helmsdale, the train turned inland as it began its path into the bleak rolling expanse of peat and boggy wetlands, with the occasional stag and hind to gaze upon. By now dusk was starting to mute all the colours and I was starting to feel a little anxious. I was banking on the fact that this far north the sun would set a lot later than down south, giving me the opportunity to cover the 16km I would still have to travel from Thurso to my first night's accommodation at Brough. Watching this darkening scenery slowly pass by, I was secretly willing the train driver to put his foot down, but it seemed that he only had one speed and that was slow.

Eventually, at 21:45, after waiting what seemed to me like hours at Georgemas Junction, we arrived at Thurso station. Hoping I had all my possessions on me, I ran out of the station and located the A836 leading to the small hamlet of Brough at the bottom of the Dunnet Head peninsular. By now, the sun was slowly setting and road traffic was starting to use sidelights. I pushed as hard as I could and after an hour arrived at my pre-booked B&B accommodation at Brough. Thankfully, my hosts were still up when I checked in. I quickly enquired as to how far Dunnet Head was away from their B&B. I was told that it was only 5km away via a narrow road. Straight away, I was back on my bike and, with only the slightest hint of daylight left, was able to cover that distance and take a photograph of the barely distinguishable lighthouse before returning for a well-earned cup of tea and the daunting thought of starting my trip proper the next day.

The following morning my wish for good weather had fallen on deaf ears. Wet and very windy conditions engulfed me as I set off on my character-building adventure. I have to admit that the thought of cycling the best part of a 1000m (1600km) daunted me and Lands' End seemed a long, long way away. Despite the bad weather, I quickly covered the 20km to John O'Groats, which is actually situated down a narrow road. I didn't want to stop longer than necessary, so took the obligatory photograph of the John O'Groats signpost, then jumped back on the bike and let the brakes off. After picking myself up, I cycled back up to the main road and headed for the coastal town of Wick – a mere 27km away. However, all too soon, as well as the inclement weather, the heavy fear of failure soon wrapped its cold shroud around me. What started out as a more than capable set of strong legs, turned out to be just hollow replicas filled with jelly. Alarmingly, the rest of my body came out in sympathy and I started to shake violently – I had hit the wall and ground to a halt.

As I stood bracing myself against the wind and rain, I thought to myself, *Is this it, is this as far as I can go – failure on my first day?* I couldn't understand why I felt so weak. Initially, I had planned to cycle the 112km to the small coastal village of Golspie but, at this rate, there was a strong possibility that I wouldn't be able to cycle the relatively short distance to Wick. In some forlorn hope, I drank the entire contents of my water bottle, hoping that it would miraculously give me renewed strength. It was obvious I was dehydrated, because after wobbling slowly for a kilometre, I started to feel better.

Eventually arriving in Wick, I found a supermarket café and sat down to a substantial meal. I was still shivering, cold and wet, but the hot meal warmed me up a little, and my mood improved. Yet, the unthinkable prospect of me having to purchase a return ticket home before I had even started this trip played on my mind. But, thankfully, on exiting the supermarket, I was greeted by the warm rays of the sun. The north-eastern side of Scotland had given me a taste of the weather which I could expect at any time, but for now, I was just grateful that the sun was shining and I was on my way.

When you hear of the Scottish Highlands, you automatically think of majestic towering mountains, but they also have beautifully bleak, undulating hills along the eastern shoreline. As I made my way slowly along the A9, the views out to the grey sea were breath-taking.

Eventually, I arrived at the village of Helmsdale, where I couldn't help but think that it sounded like a fictional battle in JRR Tolkien's *The Lord of the Rings*. I just had visions of 10,000 Orcs grunting and snorting as they came running over the nearby hill to slaughter everyone and everything in sight, but in reality, all I saw was a large rabbit in a field (don't laugh; it could have been a Rhosgobel rabbit!).

Apart from my vivid imagination, the afternoon passed by without any incidences. The road traffic was courteous and, with a huge sigh of relief, I eventually made it to Golspie.

Now, seeing that this was the beginning of July, there were certainly no guarantees that I could secure suitable accommodation every night. This obvious weak link would always be an issue at this time of the day. My confidence was always high, but approaching any destination, doubts would always creep in. I didn't have an initial plan; I just thought that the best method of securing suitable accommodation would be to enquire at every opportunity with the adage of the first available one would be the best one. With that in mind, the first one I called in was the Ben Braggie hotel and, low and behold, a single room was available – great news.

Later in the bar, after finishing a tasty meal, I was surprised that I had generated such an interest. I thought that End to End cyclists would be a common sight – even to the extent of being a complete nuisance on the roads, but this was never the case.

By 08:45 the following morning, I was back on the road, suitably lathered with copious amounts of udder cream to soothe my tender derriere. The road and weather was good, with the occasional gradual climb to negotiate. I kept to the A9 and had a fantastic downhill ride on the dual carriageway into the historic city of Inverness. Riding on dual carriageways is safe enough, if you keep to the hard shoulder. However, when you do keep to the hard shoulder, you must be aware of the potential risk of punctures. On this small metre-wide strip of tarmac, all kinds of small sharp objects linger, each one with the determination to shred or at least puncture your tyres with the least provocation.

I would have liked to stop for a while in Inverness, but could not afford this luxury with a tight time schedule to keep. Anyway, cycling along the famous and beautiful Loch Ness was recompense enough.

After 112km, I had arrived at the pretty village of Drumnadrochit, popular with Nessie-hunting tourists. Although finding Nessie would have been quite cool, securing accommodation took priority over this fabled monster. Luckily, I found a B&B, three doors down from a pub, where that evening I tucked into a fine meal of venison.

With my general fitness improving, along with the reduction of protests from my legs and lungs, the road to my next destination of Glencoe was stunning. The remainder of the ride along Loch Ness was spectacular as I made my way to and through the popular village of Fort Augustus. Approaching Fort William, I suddenly realised that, without knowing, I had cycled past the highest mountain in the UK. Yet, there was no sense of its towering majesty. I had half-expected to see the glorious 1345m body of Ben Nevis silhouetted against the blue sky, but all I saw was a sign stating the Nevis range. Far more helpful would have been a great big Monty-Python-style finger poking out from behind a cloud. This would easily indicate to everyone who wanted to know the exact position of this erosion-resisting lump of granite but, disappointingly, only the faint remnants of a distant aeroplane's vapour trail was visible in the sky and that was heading completely in the wrong direction.

The remaining 28km hugging the narrow part of Loch Linnhe to Glencoe was a joy to cycle. Yet, as I approached the village, which is aptly described as having "soaring, dramatic splendour", the large iron and concrete bridge crossing over the entrance to Loch Leven was, to my way of thinking, incongruous and completely spoiled the area's natural beauty. I'm sure someone could have designed this bridge more sympathetically and in keeping with its awesome surroundings. I turned off the main road into the older part of the village, hoping that it would be more popular and therefore have more B&B opportunities and, luckily for me, I was successful on my third enquiry.

Later that evening while having a meal at the local inn, I read more about the infamous Massacre of Glencoe. Apparently, in 1692, over 30 members of the Clan MacDonald of Glencoe were killed by forces acting on behalf of the government of King William III. The Clan MacDonald had fed the soldiers and given them shelter for nearly two weeks before the soldiers turned on their hosts for allegedly failing to pledge allegiance to the monarch.

The following morning, after quickly scanning the area for any of King William III's Scottish government forces, I continued out of the village on what I believed to be the old road, which re-joined the A82 at Loch Achtriochtan. The next 8km was a gradual climb up through the narrow glen with each side lined with ancient, impressive and solid-looking mountains, making me feel so very small and insignificant with their ineffable beauty bearing down on me. But all too quickly, like an old person not wanting to keep you too long, the glen soon waved goodbye as I free-wheeled down on the smooth twisting road leading to the bleak, empty and large expanse of Rannoch Moor.

Now, if you like boggy, open moorland, then Rannoch Moor's, 130km² of wilderness is the place for you. It is stated that its location is where the last great glacier in the United Kingdom lay, and as a result it is still rebounding back at 2-3 millimetres each year. As much as I wanted to stop and explore this unique terrain, the sooner I started this battle against a strengthening headwind, the better. Even with this enthusiasm and the numerous lochs and lochans to keep me company, it was still a long hard 42km to Crianlarich. Luckily, arriving there, I was allowed to eat lunch at a rather posh-looking hotel. Maybe the sight of a windblown MAMIL wasn't as off-putting as I expected it would be.

From Crianlarich, the reward for battling across Rannoch Moor was a 12km gradual descent into the Loch Lomond and Trossachs National Park with a stunning cycle ride along the beautiful, tranquil Loch Lomond. It states that the loch lies on the Highland Boundary Fault and is often considered the boundary and gateway between the Lowlands of Central Scotland and the Highlands. It's amazing how a vista of such beauty can take away all of your aches and pains. It doesn't matter how much you are suffering, mentally, or physically, a slow cycle ride along a lake or loch can melt away any discomfort and anxiety felt.

All too soon, I arrived at the southernmost point of the loch at the pretty village of Balloch. My fears of finding accommodation were soon quelled after securing a room at the Lomond Park Hotel. Although I'm not a football fan, I couldn't help but hear the mounting excitement emanating from the bar.

On closer inspection, I found everyone cheering at a large wall-mounted TV screen. I half-expected to witness the intense rivalry between two Scottish Premiership sides, but it turned out to be a World Cup match of equal intensity (I can't remember who played, or who won, because I found a quieter corner, finished my drink and went to bed).

The next leg of my journey would be a long 139km section to Thornhill, a village south of Sanquhar and north of Dumfries. But to get there, I had to first negotiate the thriving port city of Glasgow. As I arrived on the outskirts of the city, I turned off the A82 onto the old Dumbarton Road. To my right was the mighty River Clyde, so very important for the world-famous Glasgow shipbuilding. It was clearly evident as I cycled towards the city centre, that the majority of the shipbuilding yards had disappeared, no doubt victims to the ever-changing world economy.

From my vantage point, the width of the River Clyde was quite daunting. I knew I had to cross it at some point, but where, I still had to discover. Crossing over it on the wide Erskine Bridge would take me away from my intended route, so I continued towards the city centre. Approaching the Clyde Tunnel, I enquired as to the crossing of it and was told that the best method would be to use the dedicated tunnel used by cyclists. However, on arrival, it was not obvious as to the exact location of this tunnel. I asked an older gentleman to put me in the right direction. This he did with a casual wave of his hand. When I looked in the general direction to which he was pointing, there were still many choices to make. So, fair play to him, when he saw me struggling with his vague directions, he walked with me to the point where I could see the entrance of the tunnel and, within a few minutes of cycling, I emerged wide-eyed at Elder Park.

From my basic map of Glasgow, I knew I had to cycle past the world-famous Ibrox Stadium. I asked several people for directions, but they were again vague with their replies (maybe they were Celtic fans?) Eventually, after weaving my way along city streets, I successfully navigated my way out of the city and on to a gradual climb up to the large town of Stewarton. From there, a headwind slowed me down all the way to Kilmarnock. Once on the A76, it was just a matter of following this road all the way to Thornhill.

Now, for some reason, I had miscalculated the mileage on this stretch. I only realised my mistake when I stopped at a café in Sanquhar and noted that Thornhill was still another 20km away. It had been a long hard ride to get here and when you think you are close to your final destination you readily relax and, as a consequence, it's doubly hard to motivate yourself to continue cycling for another hour or so – and knowing my luck, it would be uphill all the way. But, thankfully, for the moment, the immediate gradient out of Sanquhar was downhill.

My logic was, in order to benefit from this downhill section, I should create as much extra speed as I could, then I would travel further up any hills before I would have to start peddling again. With this intricate plan still fresh in my mind, off I took, with as much speed as my tired legs could muster. The newly laid tarmac helped make it even faster as I leaned left and right, speeding around sweeping bends – head down and tucked in on the straights. The cycling Gods must have been with me, because not once did a rouge hill jump out in front of me and force me to climb over it, and before any other hills woke up to my presence and put me in my place, I arrived in Thornhill.

The next morning, continuous rain accompanied me all the way to the bypass of the market town of Dumfries, where even the hot interior of a fast food outlet couldn't prevent me from shivering uncontrollably. So, before departing and in a desperate attempt to warm up, I went into the toilet and stood as close as I could to the automatic hand dryer, in a feeble attempt to warm up before moving off in the direction of Gretna Green. Not long after, a large articulated lorry from a town close to where I live overtook me. That sudden recognition of a familiar name made me feel a little homesick and jealous of the fact that the driver could be home in approximately six hours, whereas I was still not out of Scotland.

After staying awhile in a small café in Gretna, I left Scotland on a small road running parallel to the M6, which took me all the way to Carlisle. From there, the lovely undulating A6 took me to the market town of Penrith. Up till now, I had secured accommodation fairly easily, but for some reason, it took five attempts before I was successful.

During breakfast the following morning, I was in conversation with two other cyclists. I wanted to know if they were on the LEJOG or JOGLE, but they informed me that they were on neither. In fact, they were crossing coast to coast, or as it is fondly known as C2C, and it would take three days to successfully complete it. Now, don't get me wrong, any cycle trip is an achievement, but I couldn't help but feel a little smug in the fact that I was on a far longer unsupported trip and was feeling good.

Feeling good doesn't always equate to good weather, because poor weather was still with me as I made the gradual climb up to the small village of Shap. On a drizzly day, Shap has little to offer and, besides, I wanted to get this exposed part over as quickly as I could and reach the summit, so I didn't stop.

Before the M6 was built, Shap Fell used to be notoriously difficult and dangerous for drivers using the A6 and as I descended, I was glad that I had come from Penrith and not

Kendal because, by the looks on the faces of the group of cyclists coming up from Kendal, their ascent seemed far worse than mine. After Kendal, the weather improved with excellent cycling all the way to Wigan. Normally, cycling 148km would be a real challenge for me, but my fitness had improved greatly.

Approaching the outskirts of Wigan, I started to look for the usual B&B accommodation signs, but all I could find were large hotels. Facing this dilemma, I knew that I would have to pay a substantial amount if I were to stay in one of them, but it would be far better than sleeping rough in a large city. So, outside one particularly grand one, I parked my bike alongside a Maserati before enquiring at reception. Predictably, I was informed that there were no rooms available, but the helpful receptionist contacted a smaller hotel not too far away where the beer was cheap and the food tasty.

The next 112km saw me arriving at the medieval county town of Shrewsbury. It is the largest town closest to Mid Wales and, as a consequence, many people I know work there and it also provides the much-needed medical services for our local health service. I was happy and relieved to arrive there. It was an opportunity to stay one night in the flat of our eldest daughter, Ceri. Staying this close to home, also allowed my wife, Sue, and our youngest daughter, Ami, to travel the 48km to join me and bring a much-needed change of clothes. Later in the evening, I swopped my tyres around; because of the extra weight of my panniers, the back tyre was getting balder faster than the front.

My next port of call was 120km south in the border town of Monmouth. It was a welcome change from the low mountains of southern Scotland, the open moorlands of Cumbria and Lancashire, and the larger conurbations in between. Now, I cycled through the soft rolling hills of Shropshire and

Herefordshire. Their neat, manicured fields a vast contrast to the wild open spaces experienced during my first week on the road.

Taking a more direct route to Monmouth from the cathedral city of Hereford, the hill at Llancloudy nearly beat me. Many people will suggest to cycle out of the saddle when the road becomes too steep – that's OK if you are not carrying excess weight – but it's not so easy if you are weighed down with bulging panniers. Nevertheless, I was determined that I wouldn't stop and walk at any time during my trip and therefore, through gritted teeth, I summited successfully and enjoyed a gradual descent into Monmouth.

It was while waiting at a set of traffic lights that I nominated myself as "Dick of the Day". At the start of my trip, I made the decision to use clipless pedals with cleats, which fit onto special cycling shoes. It states that they give you more efficiency, with more of your energy going to each pull up and push down of the pedal stroke. This creates a constant application of power through each rotation. Also, everything is in alignment, which could reduce ankle, knee, and hip injuries. However, the most important rule you must follow is the twisting of your feet to unlock the clips before coming to a complete halt. By now, I was more than adept at this manoeuvre; in fact, I needed only to unclip my left foot and keep my balance canted to the left while motionless. It was at this point at the traffic lights when my adeptness deserted me completely. As I straightened up to ease my aching back, my point of balance went past the vertical and before I had the chance to unclip my right foot, I found myself floundering recumbent on the road surface. It must have brought a smile to the faces of the people in the queue of vehicles immediately behind me. No doubt, all of them with the opinion of, *what a dick*. After nursing my grazed kneecap,

I found a lovely old pub in the town square and settled down to a relaxing evening.

From Monmouth, my next leg of the trip would hopefully finish in the historic market town of Taunton. But first, I had to cycle alongside the beautiful wood-lined River Wye and past the famous Tintern Abbey. This huge structure looked majestic as the morning sun broke through the mist and drizzle. Bypassing Chepstow, the wide Severn Estuary came into view. Apparently, it is one of the most important estuaries in the UK for wintering water birds, especially swans, ducks and waders, but in truth my goal was to cross the 1600m long Severn Bridge as fast as I could, leaving the bird-watching for another day. Once over the bridge, I called into a fast food outlet, but I have to admit that it was the worst meal I have ever tasted. I wasn't even sure if I was eating the contents, or the packaging. It was a bland, tasteless meal which I left half-eaten and vowed never to return.

Cycling along the estuary, it was a nice, easy ride to Avonmouth. But the road into Bristol, with the narrow gorge and the increasing traffic, was quite intimidating, particularly riding along the Avon River and under the slender-looking (is that strong enough to stay up there?) Clifton Suspension Bridge. No doubt there were cycle routes purposely made for cyclists to negotiate this part of Bristol. All I knew was that I wanted to be on the road which passed Bristol Airport. So I half-ran, half-skipped across the many large roundabouts and junctions to finally access the steep Bridgewater road up and out of Bristol.

Once over the AONB known as the Mendip Hills, it was an excellent ride across the 650km^2 flat expanses of the stunning Somerset levels. Now, some people will think that continuously cycling on a flat surface would be an ideal ride. However, I find that continuous pedalling in one position without any respite can have a negative effect on your body. If you are climbing, then your body is in different position and after the climb you then reap the reward of freewheeling down the other side. So, in reality, I find it better to have a mixture of gradients throughout the day.

My original destination was Taunton but, on arrival, I couldn't find any vacancies. So I kept on cycling and enquiring at every opportunity. At one point, I was even considering suitable bus shelters to bed down in. Luckily, on my ninth attempt, and after a total of 153km of backside-numbing cycling, I secured a room at the Beambridge Hotel near Wellington. It was expensive for me at £50 per night, but I was so very grateful to have a very tasty meal inside me and a soft bed to sleep on.

It was a good ride to the historic town of Tiverton and on the map, the road to the market town of Crediton looked OK, but in reality, it was quite hilly, but you have expect it in this particularly beautiful rural part of the county. Most of the A30 was OK, with stretches of gradual climbs and gentle descents. I found accommodation easily at the White Hart Hotel in the ancient town of Launceston.

While in conversation with the locals, it was suggested that, due to the inclement weather forecasted, it would be far more sensible to cycle around the spectacular Bodmin Moor, instead of cycling over it. For once, the weather forecast was correct and I was very glad of the advice to cycle on the A39. To have cycled over Bodmin Moor in such stormy conditions would have been foolish and downright dangerous. By skirting around it, I had evaded the brunt of the stormy conditions. I re-joined the A30 at Indian Queens but, to my dismay, the stormy weather had increased in intensity. This main arterial route to Penzance was very busy. The bypass around Redruth was particularly difficult, with the treads of large tyres on large vehicles doing what they were designed to do and that is to displace copious amounts of water in my general direction. Together with this thorough drenching, turbulence and poor visibility, this made the cycling – even on the hard shoulder – particularly unpleasant. At one point, there were large road works, with temporary road signs requested cyclists to find alternative routes. However, having no knowledge of the immediate area and being so wet and cold, plus no chance of referring to a paper map, I just wanted to get to Penzance as fast as I could. So I completely ignored them, much to the annoyance of the road maintenance crews.

At last, my goal was in sight, but for some unknown reason, Penzance had forgotten to put the bunting out for me. As a result, no one took any notice of me as I blew in.

My original plan was to cycle the 16km to Lands' End and back in the remaining hours left in the day, but the storm had put paid to any notions of continued cycling and, to tell you the truth, I just wanted to get out of the storm. My heart sank as I approached the first guesthouse. A large "No Vacancy" sign stood defiant in the window. Nevertheless, I still knocked on the door and before the landlady could utter the words "can't you read the sign", I asked her for alternative accommodation in the town. She graciously suggested that I make my way along to the nearby popular quayside area, but as I cycled around an exposed corner, I was met by the full force of the storm and was nearly blown off my bike. Any thoughts of cycling from there quickly evaporated and I was forced to walk.

Surprisingly, I was successful on my first attempt. Yet, as I stood there knocking on the door, looking like a drowned rat, my hopes were not high, but she just said, 'Come in and bring your bike.' I informed her, that both the bike and I were in no fit state to come in, but all she said was, 'its only water.' I liked her straight away.

Later that evening, I met a fellow guest in the hallway. We both were going out for a meal and decided that we would go together. His name escapes me now, but I remember that he came from the Chester area and was walking the coastal path. We found a nice pub and settled down to a meal.

Now, anyone who knows me well knows that I have a stammer. When I was young, it was a problem, but over the years I have learned to deal with it and now it only trips me up occasionally. Unfortunately, my companion for the evening had a severe stammer. I do not want to make light of any person who suffers from any speech impediment, but having overcome mine, I found the irony of trying to converse with him throughout the evening a little amusing, with me trying not to be influenced by his stammer and regressing back to my younger days.

After a leisurely lie-in, calm conditions greeted me for my last push and finally the completion of my trip. The short journey to the rugged and beautiful Lands' End was made even easier with no heavy panniers to weigh me down. It was with a spring in the step that I made my way up and past the ticket office and on to the Lands' End retail complex. Behind this lay a hotel and small cottages and finally after 12 or 13 days of unsupported effort, the majestic and rugged Cornish coastline revealed itself to me.

To celebrate this achievement, I asked two ladies if they would be so kind and take a photograph of me in front of the fingerpost. I hoped that this request would generate many questions about my awesome trip, but after taking two pictures, all they said was, 'Oh well done, dear,' and moved off. It was at that point that my shoulders sagged and my balloon, which was full of pride, slowly deflated – obviously, it wasn't on their to-do list. That small setback didn't prevent me from enjoying a leisurely sun-filled return journey back to Penzance.

Now, because my panniers were only showerproof, the only way I could have a chance of keeping my clothes dry was to keep them in two plastic bags inside the panniers. But on arrival back at the guesthouse I was humbled to discover that the landlady had tried to lay out some of my manky clothes that I had left lying around, in a vain attempt to dry them out (she must have had a very strong constitution because I'm sure it wasn't the most pleasant of tasks).

Luckily, my room was available for two nights. So, for the rest of the day, I strolled around the town. This felt quite strange, having for the last 12 days tried to cover as much mileage as I could in the shortest length of time. I felt quite guilty, slowly perusing the antique shops and relaxing quietly in characterful pubs. It seemed that my mind still needed motion, but my body had definitely come to a standstill.

Thoughts on the train

On the long train journey back home, I had many hours to reflect on my End to End trip. To be honest, I'm not sure how I felt. It had been an ambition of mine for many years, yet I didn't feel a great sense of achievement. I thought I would have been elated by my trip. Maybe that throwaway comment from those ladies who took my photograph the previous day took some wind out of my sails – who knows?

I thought I would be exhausted after cycling nearly a 1000 miles but, in reality, I was as fit as the proverbial butcher's whippet. In fact, I had found it quite easy. There were no ill effects on my part and the bike had supported and transported me without any mechanical problems. Most of the drivers had been very courteous, giving me a wide berth whenever they could. Strangely, I did think that I would have seen more cyclists on the same quest as me, but I rarely saw any.

This anti-climactic feeling lasted until I was nearly home, when I accepted the fact that someone's achievement doesn't always mean as much to others. Let's face it, the main winners of this trip was the Air Ambulance, who benefitted to the tune of £680. Obviously, all the people who supported me and sponsored me thought it was more than worthwhile and with that in mind, the biggest smile spread across my face.

If you have the chance of completing the End to End, whether supported or unsupported, I'm sure you will have a great sense of achievement and hopefully some good cause will benefit from your efforts.

Turn left at Dunkirk – 2011

Bruges

After such a successful End to End in 2010, I decided to embark on another long-distance cycle trip. This time I decided to cycle solo from Dunkirk, through Belgium and Holland, up through Germany to Denmark. These Northern European countries were a complete departure from our usual sunny destinations on the northern coast of the Mediterranean Sea. Like many people, we have our favourites, which include France and Italy. Many of the other countries we have only seen fleetingly as we journeyed through, or returned through. To access these countries, we tend to use the Dover/Dunkirk crossing more because it uses more freight traffic and, as a consequence, it's cheaper than the Dover/Calais route. In fact, we had only two weeks previously disembarked at Dunkirk to drive the long journey down through France to Nice and then a crossing over to the beautiful island of Corsica. It was while waiting to depart from Dunkirk after that fantastic, if rather tiring, holiday that I thought it a little daunting to think that, in one week's time, I would be returning once again to Dunkirk and the starting my Northern European cycling trip.

I like driving on the continent. It gives me a lot of freedom and to a certain degree feeds my appetite for some sort of adventure. As for Northern Europe, it was only an area where, a few years previously, I had just driven through as part of our return journey from Northern Italy. On a bike, I felt excited with the prospect of exploring these countries at a slower pace.

So, at 06:25, I left Newtown station en route to Dover. Every train was on time and the channel crossing to Dunkirk was smooth. From the ferry terminal, I knew there was a 33km ride to the Belgian border and a campsite I had researched for my first night. So, after disembarking I headed for the centre of Dunkirk on the small road, Route des Dunes, which runs parallel to the sea.

Like the D-Day landings on the Normandy coastline, this part of France saw fierce fighting during World War II when Allied soldiers were evacuated from the beaches and harbour of Dunkirk. Frustratingly for the admiralty, Dunkirk's beach was too shallow for the Royal Navy battleships to safely approach in order for them to attempt a rescue. So, between 27th May and 4th Jun 1940, approximately 700 UK civilian boats of various sizes helped transport troops to battleships waiting out in deeper water in the North Sea. Today, none of this traumatic history is apparent to me as I cycle alongside this area full of sand dunes and oil refineries.

As usual, in order to navigate through the various regions and countries, I had printed off several maps with the notion of discarding them en route. This plan worked well as I slowly navigated my way through the centre of Dunkirk. I located the D60, a small coastal road which would hopefully lead me to the Perroquet campsite I had targeted on the Belgium border. By now it was early evening and the warm sun had been replaced with a cooling sea mist as I cycled into the campsite. So, after checking in, I erected my small tent on a lovely flat manicured pitch and then looked around for a bar to relax in. I had noticed a local tabac at the end of the road leading to the campsite, so I walked the 200 metres there and settled down.

Due to my previous cycling experiences in France, I wasn't surprised to discover that the tabac closed at 20:00. So, as I headed back towards the campsite, I called in at a restaurant hoping for a nightcap. What a piece of luck this turned out to be because, unbeknown to me, I had walked into the middle of a French stag night. A crowd of already enthusiastic rugby players had dressed up as Tour de France cyclists and were noisily enjoying themselves. Now, seeing I was still wearing my cycling jacket, I was greeted with a huge cheer and spent the next hour drinking and banging the table to the sound of fantastic accordion playing and raucous French rugby songs. What a fantastic first day.

The next morning my plan was to cover the 126km to Stekene, which is located in the Belgian province of East Flanders. To achieve this, I would follow the 511 cycle path heading for Bruges, but the signage at various junctions was very misleading and, as a consequence, I got hopelessly lost and entered Bruges from the wrong direction. However, this was not all bad because these poor directions forced me to cycle through the centre and admire the beauty of this historic city. Having no real luck with the designated cycle route,

I completely gave up on the suggested 511 route and followed the cycle path which runs alongside the main road all the way to Stekene. This made navigation easy and with a flat terrain, I soon arrived at my next campsite.

It was a friendly site and after a very tasty meal and a few drinks I returned to my tent for an early night. However, this didn't go entirely to plan, because in my haste to secure a pitch, I had inadvertently pitched close to a children's play area and at this time of the early evening, all they wanted to do was vent their energy by screaming as loudly as they could at the smallest interaction. I have to admit that this loud intrusion into my early night did annoy me a little, but after a stern word with myself, I accepted the fact that they were just children enjoying their holiday and in a way I wished I had some of their energy to take with me.

My next target was to cross the border into Holland and head for the port city of Antwerp. I had tried to persevere with the designated cycle route but, true to form, I got lost again. I had found it difficult to find roads big enough for a cycle path to be positioned alongside them that was going in the direction I wanted to go. Many of the roads around the area were motorways and completely off limits to me. Now, this might sound like a contradiction, but I really do have a good sense of direction and I quickly sensed that I was deviating away from Antwerp. Luckily for me, a couple of cyclists out for a nice slow bike ride put me right. They suggested that I stop following this particular cycle path, turn around and take a more direct route by following the motorway to the city. This suggestion seemed strange to me, but as I neared the motorway, I could see a small side road running parallel to it. This was ideal and their strange suggestion turned out to be sound advice and the rest of the journey was incident-free.

Anticipating the difficulty of navigating through large cities, I had printed off detailed maps of the city centres. Now, Antwerp has the large Scheldt River running through the centre of it and on my map it showed two bridges crossing it but, as I approached, it was quite evident at this point that the river was devoid of any bridges. My puzzled look caught the attention of a road worker and he told me that there were no bridges, only tunnels, and the one I wanted was called the St Anna's Tunnel and accessed by a wooden escalator. This conveys pedestrians and cyclists down two flights and through a tunnel under the river to the other side. I thought *what an ingenious method of transporting pedestrians and cyclists safely across the river.*

Apparently, Antwerp is famous for the diamond industry, but seeing that window shopping would be the only viewing I could afford, I pressed on. After navigating across Antwerp I stopped at a roadside restaurant for a cup of tea in the centre of the pretty town of Brasschaat. It is stated that, in 2006, it won the award for the most liveable municipality in the world. I have to admit that it looked pretty enough, but it seemed to me just like any other town. Obviously, I wasn't looking hard enough.

Within 14km I had entered Holland. I quickly skirted around the fortified cities of Breda and the once wool capital of Tilburg.

Cycling along these Dutch roads was a complete dream, with smooth designated cycle tracks running alongside the A roads. This enables you to cycle between cities without going out of your way, which is completely different to the UK, where they send you on the least direct and the most poorly maintained route they can think of.

At 127km a campsite close to the town of 's-Hertogenbosch was my target. Unfortunately, when I arrived, the campsite reception had closed at 17:30. However, a small notice on the reception door gave a contact number. I did try accessing this number, but either my mobile wasn't setup properly, or the number was incorrect. Either way, I wasn't able to contact anyone to check in. Luckily for me, a woman who was a resident staying at the campsite, passed by and on seeing my predicament, she very kindly suggested pitching my tent amongst the pine trees at the back of her chalet. Mind you, one good thing; the bar was open and just to finish off the evening, on my return to my tent, the lady came around with a plate of food (what an angel).

After a good night's sleep and feeling refreshed, it was very pleasant cycling along tree-lined lanes as I made my way to the fortified city of 's-Hertogenbosch. Prior to my trip, I had studied my maps and I thought that this next stage after 's-Hertogenbosch would be very difficult to navigate due to the confusing amount of routes available but, surprise surprise, it was one of the easiest.

Due to their large size, I thought it better to bypass the ancient cities of Nijmegen and Arnhem where, during WWII, both were strategically important for both the German and Allied forces.

By 16:15, after crossing the beautiful flat lands of North Brabant, I arrived at the large town of Deventer. I located my campsite without any problems and soon pitched up. It was while I was erecting my tent that I drew the attention of a fellow cyclist. We exchanged pleasantries and stories of our own trips. However, he was not impressed with the tyres I had chosen to use and told me in no uncertain terms that I would have many punctures. He advised me that, in future, it would be far more prudent of me to fit Continental tyres, if I was to avoid the inevitable. His comments did make me think about my choice of tyre, but quickly dismissed it as I went for a shower.

By now, it's early evening and I was eager to find a suitable restaurant in the town. Unfortunately, between me and the town centre was a large river. The only bridge I could see to use was a considerable distance away. But, on closer inspection, I noticed a small ferry been used to transport people like me across the river, so I handed over the nominal fee and hopped on board. I stopped at the first restaurant I came to and was tucking into a tasty meal by 18:45. After the meal, I stayed there relaxing with a cold drink. It was a popular place for diners, and before long my stomach started rumbling again as I watched others tucking into large bowls of mussels. It made me realise that my body was burning more calories than I was supplying. So, I ordered a plate of assorted breads to dampen my noisy rumblings.

Seeing it was still light, I left the restaurant and decided to take a stroll around the town square. It was all very interesting, but the desire for a bar was stronger and so I found one where, oddly enough, the ceiling was covered with alpine skis (no doubt eagerly awaiting the start of the new Dutch downhill season!).

The next morning was brilliant for cycling, until I came to the former textile town of Almelo. Frustratingly, I couldn't navigate my way through this town. No matter how hard I tried, I kept getting lost. So, I stopped in the town centre to decide what to do. Luckily, at this moment, a bank clerk came out of a building to show a customer how to use the bank's ATM. Hoping that this clerk could speak English; I asked him the best way to cycle to the German town of Nordhorn. Unfortunately, he was new to the area, but quickly stopped and asked an elderly gentleman who was cycling slowly past. This retired gentleman was fantastic and seeing that he could not give me the directions through the medium of English, he promptly jumped back on his cycle and bid me follow him through the many twists and turns before arriving at a point on the side of a canal. There, he repeated the words "wasser" and "links" while gesturing with his arms to indicate that if I kept the water of the canal on my left at all times, I would safely reach my destination. What a gentleman.

His directions were spot-on and I was soon eating at a famous fast food outlet for lunch in Nordhorn, before arriving in Lingen. It was at this point where I hoped to take the road to my next campsite in Haselunne but, for some reason, I took the wrong road. It was several kilometres before I realised that I had gone wrong. Angrily, I consulted my map and hopefully chose an alternative route which would correct my mistake. However, I still wanted to be certain, so I stopped this gentleman, hoping he would confirm my choice of road. He wasn't in the mood for small talk and curtly said, 'Ja.' That should have been enough, but stupidly I still wanted him, for some reason, to elaborate more. So I showed him my map and with a deep frustrated breath, he looked at it and said, 'Ja.'

Despite this 20km detour, I still made good time and easily found the large campsite on the outskirts of the town. Within a few minutes, I was pitching my tent in the middle of their very large flat overspill field. It was while I was securing my tent that I started talking to a German father and son who were casually knocking a badminton shuttlecock back and forth. He was intrigued to discover the nature of my trip and wished me well for the remainder of it. On my return from the camp restaurant later that evening, his family called me over to their caravan and invited me to spend a very pleasant evening talking and drinking with them. They were from the ancient city of Cologne and had stayed in Haselunne during their honeymoon.

The next morning, for the first time on my trip, I was greeted with heavy rain. Luckily, I had pitched my tent on a slight mound and therefore only a small amount of water had seeped in during the early morning. Now, I must have looked a sorry sight trying to keep everything as dry as I could whilst striking camp, because the German family from the previous night took pity on me and insisted that I had breakfast with them and their three sons inside their caravan. After a hearty breakfast of cold meats, cheese and bread, I bid them farewell and set off in the driving rain on the 105km section to the town of Delmenhorst, situated just south of the city of Bremen.

Now, most of the time the cycle path ran conveniently alongside the main roads, but difficulty arose when, due to large junctions and flyovers, the path had to deviate through certain towns and villages and, to add to my growing frustrations, gave little evidence or signs informing you of how to re-join the main road. Although I asked for help at every turn, I frequently had to test many roads, lanes and streets before finding the correct one to take.

On the outskirts of this one particular town, I asked this elderly gentleman for the correct route. He gestured in the general direction of a small road, which led across open fields to a small junction. Arriving at the junction I stopped and asked myself the question, *do I turn left or right?* I could hear the main road humming away in the distance to my left. It seemed obvious to me that I should head in that general direction. So I turned left. Immediately, I heard shouting behind me and there in the distance was the elderly gentleman waving his hands and pointing for me to turn around and go right. I felt like stuffing him in one of my panniers and using him as a very efficient form of satnav. He certainly saved me from many unnecessary kilometres.

There were no real issues finding my next campsite at Delmenhorst. It was located in a lovely wooded area and looked to be a former farm, with large redbrick buildings housing the showers. It seemed a large campsite, with the bar and restaurant built to resemble an old Tudor-style building. With this type of quaint charm, I thought that it should have been much busier, but it must have been out of their holiday season because I had the site more or less to myself. Stupidly, I chose to erect my tent close to a large broad-leafed tree which, at that time, seemed OK. However, during the night, thunder storms started circulating around. There were many times when I thought I would have to get up and strike camp and move further away, but thankfully as the hours passed by, so did the storms.

After a restless night, my next port of call was 111km away at a campsite at Wischhafen. From there I would take the ferry on the three-mile crossing of the Cuxhaven to Hamburg estuary to Gluckstadt. But first I had to make my way the 13km to the city of Bremen, made famous by the Brothers Grimm's fairy tale, "Town Musicians of Bremen". Luckily for me, it was fairly straight forward because, after crossing the main bridge over the river Weser, it was only a matter of turning left and following the river out of the city.

It wasn't long after that I encountered my first very angry German male driver. I was cycling on the cycle path alongside a main road, when I approached a large junction. Now, one of the fascinating aspects of these dedicated cycle paths is that they can have their own sets of mini traffic lights especially for cyclists. This setup is most probably very frustrating for the motorists who have to stop at two sets of lights before entering the junction. As I came up to the lights, they turned to red and I slowed down. A Porsche 911 convertible had already stopped at these mini traffic lights waiting patiently for the lights to change for him, but seeing he was still stationary I took the opportunity to nip across in front of him before he started to move. He did not take kindly to my opportunistic move and started to shout at me. I took this torrent of German expletives squarely on the shoulders as I disappeared out of view. I thought that that was the end of the matter but, after the junction, he came down the road I was cycling along and he was obviously still incensed with my cheeky manoeuvre, because he was still shouting and shaking his fist at me. I was very glad at this point that the cycle path did actually deviate away from the side of the road and I was on a path he could not follow (remind me next time never to piss off a German driver).

After checking in at the campsite in Wischhafen, I sat down at a table in the spacious site restaurant. Now, one of the most stimulating parts of my solo trips was to try to communicate with the local people. This I did through learning odd words and phrases and gestures, but this strategy did not equip me with the necessary knowledge of reading German menus. Many European menus have English subtitles or, because the English language is closely connected to the French language, you can have a guess at them. However, I have no working knowledge of German and as a consequence; I had no clue as to the nature of the contents. So, I just pointed to a particular part of the menu, and was relieved to tuck into a tasty meal of shrimps, potatoes, egg and salad.

The following morning, I had to wait 30 minutes before the small ferry was available to take me and others across the estuary to Gluckstadt. I have to admit, I was a little impatient when the ferry stopped midway across. Surely they must have known that I was on a tight time schedule? It was only then when the large bow of a huge container ship passed in front of us and out to the open sea that I realised that this was the main shipping lane to and from the busy port of Hamburg.

From Gluckstadt, my next destination was 104km to the colourful coastal town of Husum. By now I was starting to travel up towards the Danish peninsular. For some reason it seemed that there were smaller roads to follow and, as a consequence, there was more intense studying of my maps – just to make sure. At one point I called in at a bakery situated in a small village to ask if I was on the correct road to Heide. The lady behind the counter confirmed that I was indeed on the correct one, but I would have to at one point turn off this road. With this in mind, I set off. Within 50 metres, I heard a shout and the woman from behind the counter was waving me to come back. Obligingly, she had drawn a sketch with all the names of the small villages that I would have to ride through before having to turn off for Heide. What a helpful lady.

After enquiring at a garage in Heide, I continued north, which, apart from a good stiff headwind, proved to be fairly uneventful.

Seeing I was close to Denmark, I thought I would treat myself and find a hotel in Husum, instead of a campsite. I found a lovely-looking hotel close to the harbour and I thought I would try out my very poor level of German. Just before stepping into the hotel, I noticed, through an archway, a group of people seated on a patio. Most of them wore black clothing therefore I automatically assumed that they were the hotel staff relaxing after a hard shift. With my shoulders pulled back and chest extended, I marched up to them and blurted out, 'Haben sie ein zimmer für heute nacht?' I hoped this to be correct for "do you have a room for tonight?" Their reply, for all I knew, could have anything from Shakespeare, to a sketch from Monty Python. I didn't have a clue – my blank expression said it all.

They quickly changed to English, having guessed correctly that I was a monoglot Brit. Apparently, they were guests of the hotel with no knowledge of the availability of rooms. Then, the lady in charge appeared and told me that rooms were available, but after giving me the prices, I decided to find a campsite instead. She suggested retracing my steps back to the outskirts of the town and cycle the 5km along the coastal road to a campsite situated under the sea defences. This was good advice, because the facilities were excellent, with flat pitches everywhere.

Having stayed at many campsites in the UK and Europe, facilities can be a lottery but here, under the sea defences, they were exceptional. It seemed there was a sporting complex attached to the campsite, with large showers and spacious changing rooms – sheer luxury. Who needs expensive hotels anyway?

The following morning I was greeted by a beautiful sunrise and knowing I was close to the end of my trip, I set off with renewed vigour. The roads were straight and flat and I soon crossed the border into Denmark. Immediately after crossing the border, I was surprised to see a large thatched property on the side of the road. This was the first and only thatched roof I had seen throughout my trip. It seemed a little incongruous to me.

After riding through the small and immaculate town of Ribe, I found a small campsite at the end of a dense wood. After setting up, I went for shower in a building which I assumed to be the shower complex. When I opened the door I was greeted by a large empty room with a toilet and cistern fixed halfway along one wall. Now, I'm no prude, but I didn't fancy relaxing on the toilet in full view of any people walking in. So, I turned around and explored other buildings.

Fortunately, the next building I popped my head into was a newly built modern shower block, with the added luxury of piped music. There was no need to rush, so I indulged in a long leisurely shower, listening to soothing music. Unfortunately, this site didn't have a restaurant, but it did have a small bar. So, I feasted on a large bag of crisps for my main and a Mars bar for dessert. This was all washed down with a couple of drinks.

If I had had more time, I could have taken the North Sea cycle path, which hugs the coastline from Dunkirk all the way to Norway. However, with the time constraints it would have taken me far too long to complete. But, seeing as it was my last day with only 30km to go, I decided to take in a small part of this picturesque coastal route. No doubt, most of this North Sea cycle path is battered by the severe weather conditions sweeping in from the sea and, as a consequence, most of the path on this short leg to Esbjerg was behind large sea defences. At one point, behind this imposing earth bank, I just stopped and listened. There was no sound other than the natural sound of the breeze and the gentle whisperings of the tall grasses swaying all around. No distant agricultural vehicle tearing up the ground, nor the distant drone of a passing aeroplane.

This makes you realise that the only thing that the modern human race as given Mother Earth is noise. Before the advent of the industrial revolution, the loudest noise that anyone could experience would be that of seasonal thunder, possibly a raging torrent, or maybe the odd volcanic eruption. Now, the whole human race makes so much noise, we have to protect ourselves from it. With most of the world's population now living in urban surroundings, the continual hum of motor vehicles and commerce is no doubt a comfort for many people. While others, who find themselves living under the numerous flight paths, are battered into quiet submission. Yet, for some inexplicable reason, even at leisure, a time when we could enjoy a moment of relative tranquillity, we still stupidly subject ourselves to loud music blasting from every conceivable device. It seems we cannot live without this artificial cacophony of loud noise to fill every moment of our lives. Lucky, I live in the countryside – albeit next to a main road, where thankfully most of the traffic is only local and from the early evening onwards – it is sensibly reduced to the odd vehicle. I know it's a modern world and I'm a part of it like everyone else, but for those five minutes I just soaked up this calming silence and was so glad I had the opportunity to savour this quiet and peaceful part of Denmark.

This final 30km to the seaport town of Esbjerg was a joy. I was very relaxed and glad I had completed what I set out to achieve. I thought in the few hours I had before boarding the ferry, I would look around this once former principal fishing port, but knowing that the shops would readily except my euros, but only give change in Danish krone, I resorted to just window shopping. Having said that, there is only so many times you can walk slowly up and down a main street just looking at window dressings before losing the will to live. So, I chose comfortable street benches to follow the slowly moving afternoon sun.

By mid-afternoon, I had boarded the ferry and had settled down to what I hoped would be an enjoyable 18-hour journey to the Essex port town of Harwich. My experience of ferries amount to the relatively short English Channel crossings and seeing I had in the past suffered from motion sickness, I was a little apprehensive about the long sailing time. However, after a tasty meal and listening to the music of the resident entertainer,

I returned to my cabin and soon fell fast asleep to the gentle sway of the boat.

Arriving the following day, I knew I would be unable to catch a train home, so I arranged to stay in a B&B on the outskirts of Harwich. This gave me an ideal opportunity to phone Sue and catch up. The rest of the day was taken up by walking around sleepy Harwich. Most of that time I felt somewhat empty, trying desperately to suppress the need for my body to jump back on the bike and continue clocking up the daily miles.

The next day, I was a little worried when I caught the early train to Liverpool Street station. It stated that unless you had a folding bike, ordinary bikes were not allowed on this early commuter train and to choose a later time to travel. However, that was not possible for me, because I needed to catch the correct train home from Euston. One commuter kindly suggested that I place my bike against the right hand door of the carriage, because all the stations into London would be accessed only from the left side. I have to admit that I was feeling very nervous when the ticket collector came around, fearful he would be a stickler for the rules and kick me and my bike off the train but – fair play to him – he just punched my ticket and moved on.

After arriving at Liverpool Street station I took on the hair-raising 5km ride to Euston station. I soon learned that the taxis and buses would continually and abruptly turn into the flow of traffic, displaying a total disregard for any other road user. Now, being the total gentleman that I am, I allowed them to cut me up without giving them the universal sign for being annoyed, because I was certain that I would come off second best if I tried to pick a fight with any of them. Despite all these hazards,

I arrived safely at Euston with very little time to relax before catching my train home.

Thoughts on the train

Before setting out, I imagined this trip would be very complicated for me. My understanding of the five different languages was pathetic to say the least. I just hoped, like every other Brit, that everyone I met would be able to speak English. Luckily, it was more or less the case with 90% of the people I met being very helpful and having a very good command of the English language.

Rightly or wrongly, it is well documented that by the late 18th century, the British Empire had spread English throughout its colonies – including America. With science, technology and commerce further cementing English as a global language, I believe it has made Brits like me very lazy when it comes to learning another language.

Another of my theories on the reason why so many people in the world can speak English is the dominance of the American music and film industry. The iconic rise of rock & roll, plus the popularity of their films, it's no wonder that that the English language is known throughout the world. Yet, in 1776, if it is to be believed, one vote gave America the English language instead of German. If that one vote had gone the other way then maybe we Brits would have a better understanding of at least the German language! Nevertheless, I was and still am very grateful that most people can understand English in order to help us Brits.

There were frustrating times when I tried to navigate my way through towns and cities and I'm sure I encountered the work of bored teenagers who turned the many cycle route fingerposts around the wrong way in order to frustrate cyclists like me.

Despite these little inconveniences, I covered the 1117km in nine days (without a puncture) and enjoyed every bit of this fantastic trip. I couldn't wait for the next one.

No Later Than 1957 – 2012

A BMW 328 competing in the Mille Miglia

I like Italy; I like the people, their food and the stunning landscape. Every town and city is overflowing with tantalizing history and what an exciting prospect to explore them in greater detail – but where? In reality, there are many breath-taking areas well worthy of exploring, but I wanted to achieve something that other people may recognise as a suitable challenge, or at least may have heard about.

It was while was watching a TV programme on Sir Stirling Moss, and hearing that he had won the prestigious Mille Miglia in 1955, that I thought that this would be the ideal trip for me. Apparently, it was an open-road motorsport endurance race established in 1927 by two young counts, Francesco Mazzotti and Aymo Maggi. It's stated that it took place in Italy 24 times from 1927 to 1957 with 13 of them before World War II, and eleven from 1947 onwards. Most of the winners had been Italians, except for two wins by Germans and the one win by Sir Sterling Moss. However, in 1957, this iconic race was banned after two fatal crashes. Tragically, the crash of a Ferrari claimed the lives of its Spanish driver and navigator, but more tragic were the deaths of several spectators who were standing alongside the course at the time.

Luckily for motorsport fans, the Mille Miglia was reborn in 1977, as the Mille Miglia Storica, a parade for pre-1957 cars, which takes several days to complete. The route from Brescia to Rome and back is similar to that of the original race, thus maintaining the same point of departure and arrival back in Brescia. In 2008, celebrity chef and fan of classic cars, James Martin, entered his stunning Maserati A6GCS. Unfortunately for him, the newly-built engine gave up under the stress and he had to abandon the parade.

After reading about this iconic route, it seemed a suitable challenge for me, but I thought cycling the whole 1610km of the parade in the time I had, was unrealistic. I thought that cycling approximately half of it, at 805km, was doable. With this in mind, I discussed it with Sue and we decided that I would take seven days to cycle from Brescia in Northern Italy, down the east coast and then cross over the central spine of the country to the wonderful capital of Rome. Then, Sue and our youngest daughter, Ami, would fly out a week later and we would have a family holiday together.

Although the idea of a romantic holiday in Rome was something to look forward to, this arrangement would mean that Sue would have to drive up to Manchester airport, which was something that she wasn't too confident about. Luckily, Ami promised to support her during the 2.5-hour journey, and then Sue would support Ami when they were in the air, because Ami's not too keen on flying. Sorted.

Now, with everything more or less arranged, I then had to concentrate on my own problems. I wanted to use my own bike, but that posed a big problem. Most of the airlines insist on your bike being boxed, but having landed, how would you dispose of an extremely large box, plus how would you find a suitable one on the return flight? To overcome this problem, I researched a Rinko bike bag. This is a large flat piece of canvas, designed by the Japanese, which can be zipped up and carried. I viewed and studied various online videos demonstrating how to dismantle my bike small enough to place in the Rinko. It seemed a bit fiddly, with me having to take off both wheels and pedals, plus turning the handles bars 90 degrees. Even then, it seemed to be a very tight fit when trying to zip up the Rinko, but it was the only option open to me, so I purchased one.

The main advantage of having a Rinko bag available at any time is that I could fold it flat enough and place it on top of my pannier rack, which is attached to the seat post of my bike. Then my small rolled up tent could be placed on top of it, and then my panniers would be placed over everything, thus preventing – in theory – anything from falling off. However, I quickly discovered that, while my bike is fairly light, it is not a state-of-the-art carbon fibre model and, as a consequence, when carrying it any distances, it felt heavy and cumbersome. I just hoped that while on the trip, I wouldn't have to carry it too far.

Eventually, the day arrived, and my friend, Clive, took me up to Manchester airport and I went through check-in and passport control without a hitch – I was on my way.

When flying, I like to sit next to the window so I can look down and try to figure out which part of the country we're flying over. This particular window seat was directly above the large conveyor belt loading everyone's luggage on board. I was anxious to see my Rinko bag being loaded, because it was an integral part of my trip and we all know about lost luggage and its consequences. I really shouldn't have worried, because there it was, on the last trolley. However, despite the many "handle with care" stickers placed by me on the bag, the baggage handlers were far less concerned with its fragile contents and unceremoniously dragged it off the trolley and threw it up onto the conveyor belt. Annoyingly, it was obvious that they hadn't eaten the required breakfast cereal to give them the strength to place it correctly on the conveyor, because it fell heavily backwards onto the tarmac. Unperturbed, they tried again to secure the bag by tossing it further up the belt. I just closed my eyes and hoped that if there was damage, then it would only be superficial.

The flight over the Alps was stunning. The awe-inspiring view of the high snowfields and glaciers made me feel very small and insignificant, plus a little sad. If the prediction of the experts on climate change is true, then this breath-taking sight could become a thing of the past and only viewed momentarily. I promised to retain its beauty in my thoughts as much as I could and wished the pilot would circle around again and give us all another spectacular view.

As the plane descended into Bergamo airport, I was a little apprehensive. Many thoughts of broken wheels and severed cables plagued me. What was I going to do if my bike was damaged? Even the smallest fracture could put my plans of cycling half of the Mille Miglia in jeopardy.

Collecting my Rinko bag off the carousel, I made my way out of the cool air-conditioned arrivals lounge and out into the oppressive heat of Northern Italy. I immediately scanned the area for a shady spot to reassemble my bike. The only place which seemed suitable to me was the large covered area immediately outside the main exit. Keeping close to the wall, I carefully placed the bag on the hot tarmac and gingerly unzipped the bag. I tried hard to ignore the various bits of bike poking out of the many rips and tears around the bag. Thankfully, apart from minor scuffs, the bike was unscathed and for the next hour I proceeded in reassembling it in front of a crowd of bemused holidaymakers.

As with most airports, Bergamo is surrounded by motorways and, as a result, completely off limits to cyclists. I knew from my maps that there was a small tunnel going under the motorway leading from the airport. After confirming this tunnel with an airport policeman, I confidently shouted "*Roma*" to him and then cycled through it and onto the quiet streets of Grassobbio. From there, I was lucky in guessing the correct road out of the maze of streets and on to a slip road that led to the motorway. Hugging the right-hand ditch, I ignored the many drivers sounding their horns and gesturing to me to turn away from the motorway, because I knew there was a slip road just before it which would take me onto an A road and away from that death trap. According to my map, this was the best road to take me the 54km to my starting point in the wonderfully nicknamed Leonessa d'Italia (The Lioness of Italy), which turned out to be the historic city of Brescia. Although there was an obvious attraction of such an ancient city, I felt that it would be too difficult for me to negotiate it at night, so I had pre-booked a hotel 9km this side of it.

I had been warned that some Italian drivers are not as courteous as they could be, so I made sure that I didn't antagonise any of them as I rode through flat productive farmland. Eventually, I arrived at a more commercial-looking area and located my pre-booked hotel – Hotel Euro Brescia. It is a large imposing modern building, which would have benefitted from a more welcoming gentleman at the reception desk. During check-in, he was quite gruff in his response to my request to have my bike securely stored in the hotel. Despite several suggestions by me, he intimated that the only way to secure my bike was to chain it to the fire escape at the back of the hotel. After doing as he demanded, I went to my room and settled in.

Later, I went into the large restaurant which is part of the hotel complex and ordered a tasty pasta meal. Afterwards, I decided to go for a walk up to a bar I had researched but, unfortunately, it was closed so I returned to the restaurant and had another couple of drinks in their small bar. Sitting at the bar, it quickly became evident that, due to the early start, plus the still oppressive heat of the day, it was time to go to bed before I made a fool of myself by nodding off.

At 09:30 the following morning, I retrieved my bike, which was still thankfully secured to the fire escape and headed the short distance to Brescia. The commercial district grew as I made my way along the straight road leading into the city. I thought it better to cycle through the centre, keeping well away from the busy junctions feeding the motorway. I hoped from there I could locate the minor road that would take me out of Brescia and towards the wonderful city of Verona. With the aid of a basic map, I followed the inner ring road and eventually found the road I was looking for. Luckily for me, the Mille Miglia museum was based on this road and seeing that huge sign on the side of the building made me feel I was truly on my way.

However, as the morning drew on, I discovered one frustrating aspect while cycling on these smaller roads and that was the many road signs for Verona guided you to the motorway. Any miscalculation on my part would surely lead to dire consequences, so I made a conscious effort to avoid them at all costs, yet, having said that, I still needed to head for Verona. So, I continued on what I thought was a road suitable for cyclists. This mistake was not really evident to me until I entered a long tunnel. For some reason there was a holdup of traffic in this tunnel and as I approached the queue of stationary vehicles, a policeman gestured to me that cycling was not allowed on this road. I didn't fancy the idea of retracing my steps back to Brescia, so I shouted that I didn't understand what he was saying and continued cycling past the blockage. When I emerged out into the bright sunlight, two police officers in a stationary police car beckoned me towards them. In no uncertain terms they announced in Italian, that I was to take the nearby slip road and leave this road immediately. Obviously, I didn't want to make a scene, but when I politely asked them if the road that they indicated was the correct road to Verona, they just shrugged their shoulders and made it very plain that I would have to work that one out for myself.

Leaving the police to wonder if I had lost my marbles for this miscalculation, I hopefully took the correct road and in an hour found myself cycling alongside the gorgeous Lake Garda. I wanted to see more of it, so I cycled a little way up the sliver of land poking its way into the lake to the small town of Simone. After soaking up the stunning vistas, I turned around and continued following the road signs for Verona. Stupidly, and again true to form, I found myself on a slip road leading to the motorway, so I had to quickly backtrack and eventually found the SR11 road leading to the city.

The campsite I had chosen was located close to the medieval fortress on top of the hill above Verona. As I made my way through the ancient city, the hill grew increasingly larger. I crossed the wide and slow-moving River Adige and made my way up to the campsite. The unpretentious entrance was a surprise. It was like walking through a hole in the hedge. There was no grand facade, just a few international flags flapping happily over a small gate and it was certainly not suitable for any touring caravans. So, with slight apprehension, I pushed my bike down the steep path to reception.

Now, some people might call this campsite unique, others cosy and romantic, while some would call it very small and cramped. I was just grateful that there was a pitch available for me – regardless of how small it was. I'm sure that it had a certain charm for the many backpackers and cyclists using it. However, if you were driving anything larger that a Fiat 500, then you would certainly need advanced driving skills to negotiate the steep narrow paths and small pitches.

Having checked in, I was shown to a communal area located on a vine-covered terrace. This afforded great views of the city below. My pitch was unsurprisingly small, but adequate. After erecting my tent, I went to reception, which doubled up as a small shop selling basic foods and drink, but it was too busy, so I decided to walk down the steep path and explore the old city below.

I'm sure that most people think of Verona as being one of the most romantic cities in Italy and famous for Shakespeare's love story, *Romeo and Juliet*. As I walked over the bridge into the old city, I tried to visualise the famous balcony from where under Romeo serenaded Juliet (I tried that once when I played the guitar under the window of my girlfriend's room, but all I got was sore fingers and a stiff neck). After walking around the narrow streets, I made my way back up the hill to the campsite and enjoyed a bottle of beer on the terrace.

Before I set off the following morning, I used their basic lavatorial facilities. As a young boy, I well remember using the shed at the bottom of the garden, but as an adult, I fail to comprehend the longevity of the squat toilet. I could understand it if I was in the middle of a poor country, but in modern Italy, I really do question the need for them. Not only is it uncomfortable to use, it is not the most accommodating when it comes to directional matters, with remnants of the previous user hanging around – seemingly waiting for some sort of applause. No doubt, it was designed to deter users like me who like to read when relaxing on the throne.

With an aching back, I cycled back down to the river, and followed it out of the city until locating the road which would take me the 102km to the UNESCO city of Ferrara. After cycling through Lombardy, Italy's richest region, the flat terrain of Emilia-Romagna proved to be a lot hotter. I lost count of the times I stopped at petrol stations and shops to buy bottles of water. For a pale-skinned Welshman, there were times when the heat was unbearable, with little or no shade to ease my suffering. Despite this, I did eventually find my way to Ferrara. I had to ask at a bakery for the precise directions to my hotel and that is where I stayed all night having a meal and relaxing.

The clear blue sky of the previous day had gone when I began the next leg of my trip. I was trying to loosely follow the route of the Mille Miglia. It's a bit like the Silk Road; it doesn't keep to the same route every year. I wasn't taking a particular route used in a particular year, but ticked off towns and cities that the parade had previously used. Therefore, the coastal town of Cervia was my next destination.

It's funny how some things stick in your mind. After I left a roadside café, a car full of young men came roaring past me, shouting as loud as they could. I thought that they were just a gang of enthusiastic young Italians and quickly dismissed it. It wasn't until I had to stop at a crossroads on the bypass of the historic city of Ravenna under large road signs clearly stating that, due to the morphing of this road into a motorway, it was clearI would not be able to continue any further. It was at this point, while thinking of what to do next, that I realised that the bungee straps securing my rucksack over my panniers were loose. As I attempted to tighten them up, I suddenly realised that my rucksack was no longer attached. Somehow, it had fallen off. Or had it? Luckily, most of the important items were securely placed in the panniers; yet losing my rucksack containing my wet weather jacket, small items of clothing, shoes and some toiletries was very annoying. I knew it would be madness to try and cycle back up the road against the flow of traffic, so I secreted the bike in a deep ditch alongside the bypass and hopefully away from prying eyes. In hindsight, leaving my bike in the ditch was stupid, but I didn't really know what to do for the better. I just hoped that by retracing my steps back up the bypass, I would hopefully find my rucksack just around the long sweeping bend of the road.

Trying to feel positive, I trotted as fast as I could along the narrow verge between the carriageway and the concrete wall erected alongside the bypass. The metal cleats of my cycling shoes making a clicking sound which echoed off the concrete barrier as I scanned the horizon for my rucksack. After a kilometre I came to the decision that my rucksack was long gone and as I turned around to walk with the flow of traffic, I tried to remember the last time I saw it. I'm not suggesting that those young lads had pulled it off when I was in the café and it was quite possible that I hadn't secured it properly when leaving the hotel that morning, but the manner in which they had mocked me as they noisily swept past me, made me more than a little suspicious.

Arriving back at the crossroads, I was very relieved to find my bike still in the ditch – unscathed. With no detailed maps showing me the route to follow away from the motorway, I decided to cycle into Ravenna and ask for directions.

Trying to find someone who could speak English is frustrating enough, but finding someone with good directional skills is even harder. With this in mind, I entered the first shop and enquired. The lady there was very helpful and gave me good directions and, after negotiating my way around the centre, I found myself approaching, albeit from a different direction, the same crossroads on the bypass. I knew there had to be alternative route, so asked a gentleman selling fruit and vegetables at a roadside stall for guidance. He immediately told me to take the small road under the bypass away from all the restrictions. Having done that, I soon found myself in a small industrial area where the noise of go-karts made me slow down. There were several men watching their protégés hurtling confidently around a twisting course, so I tentatively approached them for directions to Cervia. One of them knew the exact route and even drew a map in my little notebook of the road numbers and villages I would be passing through. By closely following these instructions I arrived at Cervia by late afternoon, and located the campsite at Camping Adriatico and settled down.

I was happy and relaxed. I had successfully completed half of my intended route and was looking forward to passing through the small town of Gambettola the following day. From there, it was onwards and upwards to the mountainous microstate of San Marino. After that, it would be a climb towards the spine of Italy and the town of Sansepolcro where I had booked a hotel.

The evening was warm and humid, with the campsite audience enjoying the outdoor entertainment of dancing and singing. Most of them were too engrossed in the rhythm and beat to notice the streaks of lightening circulating around the top of the nearby mountains. With one eye on the dancers and one on the sky, I just hoped that this particular storm would move away from my intended route.

Frustratingly, all my hopes were dashed at around 06:00 the following morning. The storm grew in intensity as the campsite slowly woke up. My small tent was no match for the torrential rain as it easily found its way inside and I had to keep mopping up the rivulets of water which threatened to dampen all of my plans for Monday. By 11:00 I had resigned myself to the fact that I wouldn't be cycling to Sansepolcro today. Not only would it be far too dangerous to cycle in such poor weather conditions, there were also reports of localised flooding. With this in mind, I thought it prudent to look for alternatives seeing that all my wet weather gear had disappeared with my rucksack.

To see which options were left open to me, I enquired at reception. I was told that I could take a bus to Sansepolcro, but they wouldn't take my bike. One other option would be to take the train, but the journey time was too long, meaning that it would be too late to check into my hotel. Another reason was that, seeing that it was a Sunday, the receptionist had found it difficult to collate all the information needed for other routes. At that moment, with all these options considered, I reluctantly abandoned my trip.

I was OK with my decision; I knew it was the correct one. Although the heavy rain had abated somewhat, it was still very windy and, let's face it, staying an extra three days in a popular coastal resort on the Adriatic isn't too shabby. I walked the 1.5km to the train station and purchased a ticket to Rome, which would see me arriving at 14:00 on Wednesday. It did cross my mind to stop at a town outside of Rome and then ride into the city as planned, but I thought better of it.

For the rest of the day, I tried walking along the seafront, but the strong wind was still whipping up a sandstorm. So, to take my mind off my abandonment, I thought I would visit the town's museum but, for some reason, it was shut. Looking around, everything looked wet and half-drowned, so I went back to the campsite and suitably drowned my sorrows.

Tuesday was much better. There was a lot of activity, with hotels and seasonal gift shops cleaning up the detritus caught in all the nooks and crannies in front of their establishments. Council workers made light work of sweeping the roads clean of stones, broken palm leaves and lightweight plastic. Everywhere I looked, I saw life was returning to normal.

Sitting out the storm the previous day, I had promised myself that I would still cycle to Gambettola, but, unsurprisingly, today it just seemed pointless and all my enthusiasm for jumping back on my bike, just like the storm, had disappeared. Even the relatively short distance of 30km to the beautiful city of Rimini couldn't persuade me to get back on the bike. I just hung around the campsite eating and drinking. They must have thought I was a good customer, or they felt sorry for me, because at the end of service in the restaurant, they gave me any deserts left over – free of charge. That perked me up a bit.

Wednesday I was up early and eager to start my train journey to Rome. I was undecided as to what to do with my small tent. It was OK in the dry, but next to useless in heavy rain. So, I popped it in the nearest litter bin. I cycled up to the station well before my departure time, because it's deceiving how long it takes to dismantle a bike and secure it properly inside a Rinko bag.

Clutching my train ticket, I made my way onto the platform. Sitting quietly in the shade, it struck me that there was only one platform, yet some passengers had walked out to a small central area in the middle of the tracks. To make sure that I was on the correct one, I asked an older woman waiting with me. She confirmed that the main platform was the correct one. She also asked if I had activated my ticket in the machine on the wall. I made out that I had a ticket, but didn't know I had to activate it. She quickly showed me what to do as the train approached. Now, I have a theory that if you ask a woman for help, especially an older one, you have a better chance of success. Older women cannot let go of their mothering instinct and quickly assumes that this pathetic-looking male in front of her requires every bit of her help. During the melee we were separated, but during the relatively short journey to the city of Bologna, she searched every compartment until she found me to make sure that I knew I had to get off this train to access the train for Rome.

Alighting at Bologna, it wasn't obvious from which platform the train for Rome departed, so my lady friend took me down to a lower level to access the larger information screen and she even asked a rail guard for confirmation. It turned out that the platform we had arrived on was the correct one for Rome. With everything sorted out, she bade me farewell. I never knew her name, but gave her a big hug and a peck on the cheek for all her help.

Sometimes I find, when you're on your own, paranoia sets in, even when you have all the information needed. Waiting on the platform, I still wasn't certain, because the end destination didn't show Rome, so I asked a younger woman and she confirmed that I was on the correct platform and stated that Rome wasn't the final destination.

At approximately 1.2m x 1.2m x 0.2m the Rinko bag is not small. With its wide strap around your shoulder and carrying any other luggage in the other hand, it was always unwieldy and cumbersome. I didn't want to leave it out of sight, so I tried to place it on the overhead racking above the seating, but a woman sitting underneath it clearly didn't think that it was a good idea. It was quite apparent that with the swaying of the train, it would very quickly dislodge itself, so I kept it as close as I could to my seat and hoped that it wouldn't block the centre aisle too much.

Two-and-a-half hours, and a little snooze, later, I arrived at the ancient city of Rome. I texted Sue to say I had arrived safely and to allow me time to reassemble the bike before trying to make my way across the city to our apartment. If Rome was a clock face, then I knew that the apartment was at 6, but I didn't have a clue where on the clock face the station was situated in order for me to cycle from. To further compound my cluelessness, there are four identical exits out of the station – *which one do I take?* I asked a man selling tickets for help. Luckily for me, our apartment was situated on the famous Appian Way and is one of the oldest and most important roads in Rome. So when I explained this to him, he gestured to one of the exits.

As I stepped out into the fierce sunshine I asked myself, *do I turn left or right?* I turned left and came to another junction. Again, left or right? I asked a shopkeeper and he said right and this was my method of zigzagging my way across Rome, asking anyone who was standing at a junction. By now it is late afternoon. I asked this one gentleman for directions to the Appian Way. His sign language was perfect. He made a circle with his arm and then pointed to his third finger and then gestured right. With this information, I continued cycling until I came to a large roundabout. There, above the third exit on the right was the street sign showing the two words I had been searching for – Appia Nuova (Appian Way).

The wide street started to slowly rise as I manoeuvred myself between pedestrians and traffic. Soon it began to descend and I gathered speed. As I approached a set of traffic lights, they turned red. Cursing my poor judgement I came to a shuddering halt. Unbeknown to me, this untimely stop turned out to be my saviour. As I was waiting for the lights to change, I looked around and started to recognise some of the buildings I had seen on Google street maps. I pulled my bike up onto the pavement and gave Sue a text. Within a few seconds I heard a shout and there was Sue waving like Juliet from a balcony high up on a tall building – I had arrived.

Our apartment was situated on the sixth floor. I tried to fit my bike into the small lift, but it was too big, so I had to carry it up six flights of stairs.

Knowing that they both had overcome their fears, I was relieved to see Sue and Ami happy. However, it had nearly turned into a disaster for them. Over a large glass of red wine, I listened to their tale of a closed, unattended, although pre-booked, secure car park. We had used this particular car park before when flying from Manchester, so I had made sure that Sue knew how to negotiate the various lanes and roundabouts of the airport. Unfortunately, when they arrived in the dark, the car park was shut. The gates were locked and there was no one in the vicinity to ask. This unexpected dilemma was the last thing they wanted. They knew they couldn't hang around for too long, so they retraced their steps back to the main road and started driving slowly. Thankfully, in this area, there are many other car parks available, so as soon as they spotted a light from another car park reception, they drove in. The gentleman quickly allayed their fears and soon they were transported to the airport. To Ami's relief, the flight was fine and the journey from Ciampino airport to the apartment was plain sailing. Directions and information from our host were very detailed and easy to follow and soon they had settled in.

The rest of the week was filled with seeing the many iconic and historic places which Rome is justly proud of. We used the frequent city buses to travel into the centre and then walk to all of the sights. There were crowds, but not enough to keep us waiting too long. Let's face it; if you have to queue for 30 minutes to enter the world-famous, jaw-dropping Colosseum, it is certainly well worth the wait. However, being from Wales, we were not accustomed to the high temperatures, which were frequently over 37°c. As a consequence, it was not possible to just wander around gazing at all the history, so frequent stops in bars helped us to adjust to the oppressive heat.

We were very fortunate to visit the Vatican on the last Sunday of the month and, therefore, admission to the museums was free. Yet, I'm embarrassed to admit that after walking around the huge expanse of St Peter's Basilica, then walking through the museum and being mesmerised by the stunning sculptures and paintings, the nine ceiling panels of Michelangelo's Old Testament events, to me, was just another wonderful exhibition. I know art is subjective, but I had been saturated by too much beauty before arriving at the Sistine Chapel and my senses were nudging overload. My appreciation for what some people believe to be one of the greatest masterpieces the world has ever seen was somewhat muted.

Not being religious, I found the architecture and structures of Rome more appealing. The walk down the Forum with Ami really gave us an insight into the majestic past of ancient Rome. The nearby Palatine Hill, which towers over the Roman Forum and the Circus Maximus, displays some of the ruins of its ancient palaces and is still an extensive archaeological site today. This peaceful, green and shaded space is reputed to be the location of the cave of the legend of Romulus and Remus. I just thought it was a brilliant place to gaze down from and immerse oneself in the ancient city of Rome.

Although the world-famous Trevi Fountain was stunning with its masterful example of Baroque architecture, it was the Pantheon to which I kept returning. It wasn't because it is one of the best-preserved of all Ancient Roman buildings and a Catholic church since 609 CE; it was the circular interior which impressed me the most. Walking beneath the fairly standard Corinthian-columned portico didn't prepare me for this vast rotunda. I couldn't prevent myself from being pulled wide-eyed into this marble womb. Looking up at the central oculus with its wide beam of light angling down to the well-worn floor, I couldn't help but wonder how it had been constructed. Even with today's technological wonders, it would still be a marvel of construction and to think that, for the last 2000 years, it's still the world's largest unreinforced concrete dome.

Having wandered around the mainstream tourist attractions for several days, a bus trip outside the city walls to the wonderfully cool San Sebastiano catacombs was definitely worth seeing. Although they're not one of the "must-dos" in Rome, they were different and very interesting. The English-speaking tour guide was very helpful in explaining the history of the third-century catacombs. The termination of the tour in the beautiful basilica above was equally interesting.

Having emerged blinking back into the searing heat, we made our way back up the Appian Way to a small café to wait for the bus back to our apartment. While relaxing in the shade, I marvelled at the construction of this famous thoroughfare, with its large flat stones still clearly visible on one half of its width. The other half was constructed of small square cobblestones on which any vehicle could comfortably drive on at speed, but driving on the larger flat Appian Way stones proved an annoyingly yet effective method of controlling the speed of low-skirted modern cars.

As with all holidays, the week passed by all too quickly and, before we knew it, we were back on the plane flying home.

Thoughts on the plane

I am very proud to say that I attempted to cycle half of the Mille Miglia but disappointed that, due to inclement weather, I was only able to complete a half of that. Maybe I was a little naïve to think that I could easily have completed the challenging route from Cervia over the mountains and still arrive in time to check into my pre-booked hotels, but that challenge still appealed to me. Having said that, I know that I made the right choice, but a little bit of me still wonders if I would have been successful.

The two hotels I had paid for but did not use in Sansepolcro and Spoleto I quickly placed in the back of my mind under the heading of "put it down to experience" and totally forgot about them.

It was great to spend time with Sue and Ami exploring as a family all the fantastic sights that the great city of Rome readily displays. Plus, I was very proud of them for overcoming their fears of driving on motorways and flying. What a fantastic combination.

If you have the opportunity, please visit this fantastic city. You'll not be disappointed.

Down Under – 2013

Perth City skyline

Australia is stated to be the largest country by area in Oceania and the world's sixth-largest country – and we love it.

In July 2007, we had been invited out by our friends, Mary and Ade, for a wonderful three-week holiday in Kwinana, which is close to the beautiful city of Perth in Western Australia. This would be my first time in an aeroplane and, although it was a long way to travel, I thoroughly enjoyed it.

Perth is a modern city and the capital of Western Australia and sits where the Swan River meets the southwest coast.

Mary and Ade were the perfect hosts on our first antipodean holiday and showed us all the sights and sounds of this vibrant city. It included art galleries, nearby wineries, boat trips up the Swan River, parks and gardens, which gelled effortlessly with the laidback attitude of the local people. However, one slight negative observation of the beautiful city of Perth is that it is remote and a long way from anywhere. In fact, one of the nearest cities to Perth is Denpasar in Indonesia at 2580km and, as a consequence, when you have seen every attraction in and around Perth, then you would have to fly a long way to experience something new.

This was foremost in my mind when, in 2013, we were invited once again to fly out to see Mary and Ade. Although there had been a lot of development in and around Perth since our first trip, I wasn't sure that these new sights would be sufficient to occupy our days for the three weeks of our stay. Like most people, I like nothing better than sitting drinking a cold beer in the shade, but there is only a certain amount of sitting outside a bar watching the parrots and pelicans flying around before my body shouts loudly in protest of this inactivity.

Before flying out, I had looked online for cycle rides in and around the Perth area, but found nothing suitable. However, my research did throw up a more challenging ride. I discovered that the 1000km Munda Biddi Trail ("path through the forest" in the Noongar language) is Western Australia's premier long-distance off-road cycling experience and meanders through scenic river valleys and magnificent forests. It starts in Mundaring, which is 30km northeast of Perth and ends in the south coast city of Albany. It uses a network of bush tracks and disused railway formations with sections suitable for cyclists of all ages and experience levels. Ideally, it's suggested that you should allow three or four weeks to complete.

Despite the obvious appeal this trail had for me, I knew it would take up the whole of our stay to complete it. And seeing as I still wanted to spend time with our friends and see the new sights in and around Perth, I knew I had to abandon thoughts of using all of our holiday time just cycling the Munda Biddi Trail. Yet, the idea of cycling down to Albany appealed to me and I hoped I could find a more direct route from Perth. After peering over various maps online, I discovered that my choices were limited and, if I wanted to cycle the more direct route, then I would have to use some of the famous Australian highways. But if I was successful, then this relatively short trip would neatly shoehorn itself on the second week of our stay, thus leaving several days each side for sightseeing. So I started to make plans.

During my previous cycling trips, it was fairly easy to find accommodation at any time and at any mileage. This was mainly due to the fact that, most of the time, I was cycling through fairly populated areas. But as I stated before, Australia is vast, so you don't have that kind luxury of stopping wherever you want to. Distances between accommodations can vary greatly, as I discovered when trying to locate suitable lodgings along my route. It became apparent that I would have to leave the highway and travel out to remote towns and villages in order to secure a place to stay. So careful planning was needed if I was to successfully complete this adventure. Before flying out, I contacted a cycle shop in Perth, which hired out suitable bikes and arranged a pick-up day for the second week.

After a long flight, we were picked up by Mary and Ade and drove the 36km south of Perth to their home in the town of Kwinana. The first week was filled with reacquainting ourselves with the local sights and sounds in and around Perth. Since our first trip to Oz, the rail network system had been extended up to and beyond Kwinana, so it was a simple task of walking the one mile to the train station any time we wanted to go into Perth. This new service also pleased Ade, because he didn't have to continually transport us about like he did during our first trip.

As the second week approached, I started to get excited. But, before I could set off into the morning sun, I had to collect my bike. So, I walked the mile to the station and hopped on the train into the city and walked the short distance to the cycle shop. There, I was presented with a very nice Cannondale road bike. It was while I was completing the required paperwork that I was drawn into conversation with an older cyclist who was embarking on a journey that included the mind-numbingly long crossing of the notorious flat, treeless, Nullarbor Plain. At 1100km, it is a journey which crosses the border between Western and South Australia and should not be taken lightly; therefore he was cycling it as part of a supported group. I did rib him gently by saying that his journey was nothing compared to my 450km unsupported journey to Albany.

Now, with all the required paperwork completed, I cycled down to the water's edge to start my return trip back up to Kwinana. Perth city has a good network of cycle paths and they guided me alongside the open expanse of the inner Swan River, then under the wide Narrows Bridge supporting the busy Kwinana Freeway. I did have to ask someone for directions when I came up to a large intersection, but I should have realised that all I had to do was to keep the train track, which occupies the centre between the two main sections of the freeway, to my left and I would automatically be heading in the right direction. Feeling a bit stupid, I slowly made my way out of the suburbs and, within two hours, had made my way back to Mary and Ade's.

After saying my goodbyes to everyone, I set off the following morning in a south-easterly direction. I had looked online at the route which would take me on the 113km to my first stop at Boddington, and it was very simple. All I had to do was head for the freeway and then follow the signs. So, after negotiating my way through expansive residential areas, I found a small cycle track which led down to the freeway. I knew from there it would be easy to follow until I met the Mundijong intersection and turned left, which would take me to one of Western Australia's oldest settlements of Jarrahdale. Cycling along the flat, wide valley was easy. The roads were wide and smooth as I made my way up to the low escarpment of the Darling Ranges. The pull up to Jarrahdale was slow as I made my way through scrubby forests and occasional farmland. Unlike the close proximity of modern development, Jarrahdale, nestling amongst established trees, has a quaint nostalgic feel about it. Old colonial-style buildings were well spread out alongside the gently twisting road, which made me feel right at home. But, all too quickly, this small town was behind me as I continued along the undulating road through the quiet Jarrahdale National Forest to the Albany Highway.

Around 50km after leaving Kwinana, I arrived at the junction and turned right onto the highway. This road had to be wide enough to accommodate the famous road trains that travel the length and breadth of this vast continent. Gone were the cycle lanes that had protected me around Perth. The only safe piece of tarmac was the metre-wide verge beyond the white road boundary markings.

I have to admit that most of the road users gave me a wide berth and I never really felt in any danger, until a car passed me and stopped on the verge further up the highway. As I approached, he pulled away, only to stop once again. He didn't seem to have any mechanical issues as I cycled up to him. It was obvious that he wanted to talk to me because he wound the window down. I didn't want to talk directly in front of him in case he had a gun or a knife, so stood opposite the door pillar, making him twist awkwardly in his seat. This white-bearded man asked me where I was going and if I needed a lift. I told him I was cycling to Boddington to meet friends (I didn't want to give him the impression that I was travelling completely alone) and that I was more than capable in cycling the remaining 60km. Now, this was probably a genuine person wanting to make sure that this lone cyclist was OK in this remote part of Western Australia, but I didn't want to take any chances and end up like the many sun-bleached remains of the numerous kangaroos who had shaken hands with the countless number of heavy vehicles and quickly peddled away before he could continue his questioning.

One unwanted aspect of cycling on this narrow piece of tarmac was that, unlike the large worn chippings on the road proper, the ones on the verge were like new and apart from being sharp, were also very bumpy. This made cycling rather painful and I had a great desire for this teeth-juddering road to end as soon as possible.

It's fascinating to think how your brain can lure you into falsely estimating the distance travelled. At home, I totally rely on my bike computer to accurately give me the distance travelled that day, but without one, I find it difficult to judge. I try to calculate distance by thinking that I can easily travel at 16kph but, annoyingly, that doesn't really compensate for the many hills you may encounter when you are moving at walking pace. I know there are many apps on your smartphones showing exactly how far you have cycled, but at the time I didn't have one, so my impatience grew as the imagined kilometres grew. Eventually, I did arrive opposite the turning for Boddington. I had hoped that the village would be close by, but on closer inspection it indicated that I would still have to cycle another unexpected 14km before I could stop and relax.

Before flying out, I had asked Ade to book all my accommodations in advance and this is what he had done, so when I arrived at the Boddington Hotel, I was puzzled to discover that they knew nothing of my booking. They suggested that it could be possible that I had been booked into the guesthouse opposite, but after knocking on their door for what seemed ages, I returned to the hotel (when I say hotel, it was nothing more than a single-story dwelling with a tin roof). Yet, fair play to them, they graciously suggested that I use one of the portacabins situated on the side of the hotel. Now, reviews of this hotel were mixed, most of them ranging from poor to average, but seeing as I didn't have a choice, I gratefully accepted their offer of one of the portacabins. On entering, I could tell that the cabin hadn't been cleaned that day, but it wasn't really dirty, I just turned the pillow around and placed a clean blanket on the bed. At least the beer was cold and the evening meal tasty.

The following morning, I cycled along a different road, which took me back up to the Albany Highway. My next stop was another 113km, to the town of Wagin. As I mentioned before, I had to again turn off the highway and head the 35km to this small town. As I turned off the highway and up the small, smooth, tarmaced road, I quickly noticed that my bike had succumbed to the very sharp chippings at the highway's edge and had developed a slow puncture. I looked in the small saddle bag supplied by the bike shop and was slightly worried that there was only one puncture repair patch and one new inner tube. I did think about fitting the new tube, but decided to see how far I could get after pumping the tyre up.

Cycling to Wagin didn't really offer anything more exciting other than occasionally passing through either thin scrubby bush, or huge fields of arable crops and, as a consequence, I quickly fell into a trancelike rhythm on the endlessly straight undulating road. However, this meditative state came to an abrupt halt as the smooth sun-melted tarmac stopped and a dirt road began. Washboard-like corrugations soon jarred me into intense concentration as I had to negotiate around large stones and potholes. These conditions continued for several kilometres before mercifully joining another tarmacked road leading into Wagin. Surprisingly, the puncture had behaved itself and I only had to pump the tyre up on four occasions.

Like the majority of small Australian towns, Wagin consisted of one long, wide main street, so it wasn't difficult to spot my accommodation for the night. This was situated on the left side just past the large colonial two-storied Palace Hotel. Thankfully, the Wagin Motel was expecting me and I was soon repairing the slow puncture in the spacious lounge of my room.

Later, I popped into the hotel and had a very tasty meal while making polite conversation with an older couple who was visiting the North Island, as people from Tasmania call their larger neighbour. Talking about place names, apparently it's stated that the name "Wagin" is derived from Wagin Lake and is of Noongar origin, meaning "place of emus" or "site of the foot tracks from when the emus sat down".

From Wagin, I joined the Southern Highway heading south on the 98km journey to the very small town of Tambellup. As before, the straight, flat highway passed through huge fields of productive arable land. One thing you quickly realise is that the majority of Australia's landscape, although not totally isotropic, is certainly uniform in most directions and, as a consequence, can be somewhat boring after a while. Therefore, after a fairly non-descript day, I arrived in the sleepy town of Tambellup.

For variety's sake, I had pre-booked a B&B property on the main road. Walking up to the front door of the 1930s-style bungalow, I noticed a note pinned to the door asking visitors to ring the number stated. I had my mobile phone on me, but I couldn't get any reception. Thankfully, next door was an old-fashioned wooden-fronted garage, so I popped in to ask for assistance. They were very helpful and stated that the proprietor only lived two minutes away and they quickly phoned him. True to their word, within two minutes a truck arrived and this gentleman checked me in. He said that I would be the only person staying there that night, because he and his wife were going on holiday that week. He then presented a fruitcake that his wife had made specially and then told me to help myself to his drinks cabinet (what a generous person). He then suggested that I pop the key back through the letter box in the morning before he abruptly turned around and drove off.

Before leaving Kwinana, Sue had asked me to contact her each night, but for some reason mobile reception was virtually non-existent. So, I tried to contact her on the house phone but didn't know the number of Mary and Ade's landline. I tried looking through the yellow pages, but soon gave up.

I had been told by the proprietor that the only pub in the village was situated down the road, but was frustratingly sporadic in the days in which it was open. Hopefully it would be open tonight. As I walked the 300m to the Tambellup Hotel, I was very relieved to see it was indeed open. Not only was I thirsty, I was hungry as well, and hoped that I could have an evening meal there. I walked into a large bar where several men were sitting and drinking. I was quickly drawn into conversation and discovered that they were mineworkers on leave from the north. I told them of my frustration with the mobile reception and was told to go outside and cross the road and walk halfway across a small footbridge leading to the centre of the village – and then stop. Apparently, this slight elevation on the bridge was the only place where a mobile signal could be found. I dutifully did as commanded and indeed found a signal and was able to contact Sue and put her mind at rest. I then went back to the pub to finish my drink. Feeling pleased with myself, I ordered another drink. At this point, the barman turned to the fridge to retrieve another frozen glass. I immediately pleaded with him to pour the beer into my original glass, because I had only just warmed that one up – much to the merriment of the mineworkers. Disappointingly, there wasn't a restaurant at the pub, only a fish and chips takeaway. I'm not really a chip fan, but beggars can't be choosers, so I ordered one of them. After finishing my drink, the short distance back to my accommodation allowed my teeth to regain some sort of normality and I settled down to eat my meal in front of the TV.

Now, in my opinion, don't go to Western Australia for the TV. I find their broadcasts rather limiting, with the majority of programmes focusing on game shows and light entertainment. So, for the remainder of the evening, I channel-hopped while munching on the fruitcake and supping the landlord's sherry.

While cycling in Western Australia, I noticed that the ground conditions were mainly made of deep, unstable sand. As a consequence, many of the domestic properties had to be built on a raft foundation. This meant that, instead of filling a trench with concrete for the walls to be built off it, a solid reinforced concrete foundation slab is placed on top of the sandy ground and the walls built directly off this. These unstable ground conditions were evident by the large cracks in the walls of the bungalow and the inability to shut most of the internal doors. This gave the interior a lopsided feel about it. This didn't bother me, because I was full of cake and sherry.

By now night had descended and it was time to choose which bed to sleep on. I had the choice of four bedrooms and thoughtfully chose a single bed so as not to make extra work for the landlord.

Having being brought up on a small remote hill farm, dark nights are not a problem, yet as I settled down to sleep, I felt somewhat uneasy. Maybe it was the eerie silence of an empty building, or the intense blackness, but something felt spooky. I opened the curtains, but that made no difference at all. I silently told myself to get a grip and to go to sleep. Out of habit, I had left the bedroom door half-open and just as I was drifting off, I heard a sound which seemed to me like a long extended "wahhhhh…", just like someone close expelling a lungful of air. I shot up in bed, my heart desperately trying to jump out of my chest. Yet, apart from that one sound, there was silence. I tried to visualise an object in the bedroom I could use as a weapon to defend myself with. I slowly pulled the bed sheets away from my body, so I could have movement to either run, or at least wildly lash out at someone or something. I tried to make out the ghostly outline of a figure in the pitch black when the "wahhhhh…" came at me again, penetrating the solid blackness. I must have unknowingly picked up some courage during the day, because I jumped out of bed to confront this intruder. I flicked the light switch on only to discover an empty room and, as I cautiously peered out the bedroom door into the hallway, an automatic air freshener on a small table opposite gave out another fragrance "wahhhhh…" What a plonker! I laughed out loud and went back to bed.

The following morning, I made myself breakfast and consumed the last of the fruit cake before setting off on the 127km to the city of Albany. It seems that Australia categorises most of its towns as cities regardless of their small size, and Albany is no exception.

I was glad of the fresh morning air as I cycled out of Tambellup. The road took me through the familiar scrubby bush before opening out yet again into the unbelievably large open arable landscape. It was on this 39km stretch of the Southern Highway, before it joined the Albany Highway, that I experienced the immense size of Australia's famous road trains. I had seen these mammoth lorries before, but not up close and personal. While cycling, I had noticed that most of the highways were built up, with a slope down to the original ground level and it was down one of these slopes I wobbled when hearing the two pulls of the foghorn behind me from one of these approaching land trains. It's frightening how much air these lorries can move when passing you. I had been previously warned that these lorries usually pull multiple carriages and cannot easily manoeuvre away from anyone using the road. So, I dutifully stood several metres away from the side of the road as this awesome vehicle sped past, covering me in a dense cloud of warm air and dust.

The rest of my journey was uneventful, passing through and stopping in occasional small towns for refreshment before arriving at the Ace Accommodation on the outskirts of Albany. It consisted of a large restaurant with a row of motel rooms behind. It was ideal for me and I quickly checked in. It had all the amenities I needed, but I thought I would still walk into the city centre for a drink. Naively, I thought it would be a short distance, but soon realised that, like every town and city in Australia, Albany is also well spread out. So, after walking a kilometre, I came upon an Indian restaurant called the Curry Leaf, so I called in and had a bottle of their beer before returning to my motel. That evening, I stayed at the restaurant and went to bed a very contented man.

After breakfast the following morning, I jumped back on my bike and cycled the 3km into the city centre. It feels odd calling it a city, because Albany has only one main road leading into it, with many smaller roads radiating away to residential areas. This main road more or less terminates at the railway station at the bottom of the sloping street overlooking the sheltered Shoal Bay.

I don't know why I did the usual touristy thing of walking up one side of the main street and then walking down the other side. I knew I wouldn't buy anything, but I did it anyway. Then, after that fairly useless exercise, I scouted for a nice pub to relax in. Having said that, I was conscious of the fact that I had my bike to look after and tried to find a pub where I could keep my bike safe. I found a large hotel halfway up the street and wheeled my bike around to the back and hopefully out of sight. In the rear entrance amongst all the empty beer barrels, a group of men stood drinking. One of them realised that I wanted to secure my bike in a position where I could keep an eye on it while drinking in the bar. He assured me that no one would dare steal my bike while they were there, so I somewhat reluctantly left it in his charge. I did go back out after 20 minutes, just to see if it was still there, which brought a curt, "I told you, no worries, mate" from the gentleman.

By now it was mid-afternoon, so I made my way back to my accommodation to sleep off those three drinks. That evening, I enjoyed another tasty meal in the restaurant before returning to my room to pack everything ready for the slightly shorter return bus journey of 413km to Perth.

The following morning I was up early to cycle to the bus station and was very relieved that the bus would take my bike. The 4.5-hour journey was pleasant enough with frequent stops to pick up and offload the many passengers using the service.

Eventually we terminated at a different part of Perth – a part I was not familiar with. Although, in reality, you can't really get lost, with the iconic cityscape with its towering skyscrapers dominating the whole city. I knew if I headed in their general direction, then I wouldn't be too far away from the cycle shop. Just to be smug, I located the shop without any problems and after dealing with the paperwork, I caught the train back to Kwinana.

Thoughts on the train

With no real navigational issues, it was an easy trip. The scenery was, at best, predictable and often quite boring. The weather was bearable and the people friendly and accommodating. All in all, I was – as the Australian vernacular states – stoked.

If you want to experience what life is like in WA, then Perth is a fantastic and vibrant place to visit. If you enjoy wide open spaces to gaze upon, then it's the place for you but, be warned, WA is approximately the size of Western Europe and, as a consequence, is very big.

Happy gazing.

A Pilgrim's Trail – 2014

A Shinto temple

Japan – what a fascinating country. There's something about its history, architecture, art, food, traditions and crafts that is an immediate attraction to me. Together with their eye for detail and the quest for perfection, it's always been on my to-do list. Now, my chance had come.

With a mindboggling number of unique and thrilling experiences just waiting to be explored, it's not that easy to decide on which area/prefecture to visit and certainly not a trip to be taken lightly. So, after researching some of the many possibilities, I came across an account of someone crossing the island of Shikoku, which is the smallest of Japan's four main islands and famous for its 88 Shinto shrines. I decided there and then that this would be the trip for me. It was short enough for me to complete it in the time available, plus it had an easily accessible coastal route, taking me from Kansai Airport to the port of Wakayama. It seemed ideal.

After the obligatory vaccinations were administered, plus a few half-learned basic Japanese phrases logged somewhere in my brain, I dismantled my bike and put it into my Rinko bike bag. Grabbing my one and only piece of hand luggage, I drove up to Manchester Airport and set off for Osaka via Helsinki.

Just before arriving at Kansai Airport, I had to fill in a form detailing where I was staying during my trip. This was a little awkward because I only had my first hotel pre-booked. I just hoped that this was good enough and they would let me through. Luckily, apart from having my bike bag and contents x-rayed, I passed through customs/security without any major problems and, at 09:30, found myself standing outside the arrival lounge with no real idea of how to proceed further.

I knew that the airport was situated just south of Osaka on an artificial island in Osaka Bay, but how to get off it was still to be discovered. I crossed the wide road opposite the exit and went into what looked to me like a large shopping mall. Luckily, there was a large information desk situated just inside the entrance. To my relief, the man behind the wide counter spoke perfect English. He informed me that I could purchase a metro ticket, which would take me quickly off the island and onto the mainland. After purchasing my ticket, I was shown an empty-looking room opposite, which really confused me, so I returned to the information desk. They reassured me that it would lead me to the Metro station. On closer inspection, I discovered that this room led to an elevator, which indeed conveyed me to a lower level and the Metro. Not totally convinced I was on the correct one, I stupidly asked four ladies who were sitting next to me and they confirmed that this Metro was the only one and it did indeed go to the mainland and the first station was Izumisano.

After alighting at that station, I made my way up to a covered walkway high above a busy main road. There, amid mild curiosity, local commuters saw me take an hour to reassemble my bike before consulting my map of the area. For this particular trip, I had decided to use my Gary Fisher mountain bike instead of my Giant Defy road bike. The gearing is better for climbing and seeing as I didn't know how steep the mountains would be, I thought it prudent to take my GF. After completing my reassemble, I could see from this high vantage point the very large Ferris wheel I would need to cycle past in order to head for the correct coastal road leading to the port city of Wakayama. I started off on the 42km leg, excited to be on the move, yet daunted at the prospect of negotiating the many roads and junctions out of the city. Luckily, all the road numbers are in Arabic numerals and easily followed.

Eventually, the tall buildings of the cityscape disappeared and morphed into urban sprawl. At one point, I stopped to look down at an outside training facility for either the police or the armed forces. Rows of young men were being put through their paces at what looked, to me, like a square bashing exercise. But, seeing as I had no knowledge of Japanese protocol, I decided not to linger too long, just in case someone might think I was spying on them and arrest me.

According to my map, I noticed that there was a motorway, plus a main road that would have taken me on a more direct route to Wakayama, but I was certain that I wouldn't be allowed to cycle on them, so I continued on my coastal route. I knew there was a ferry leaving Wakayama at 13:40 for the city of Tokoshima on the island of Shikoku and I wanted to catch it. Therefore, I didn't waste too much time stopping to take in the wonderful scenery along the coast.

As I approached the outskirts of Wakayama, I was looking for the bridge indicated on my map that would take me across the estuary and into the city proper. I was sure that such a large bridge would easily be seen at this distance – yet no bridge appeared. I started to doubt my map-reading skills and in a desperate attempt to find this bridge, I stopped this unfortunate woman who was walking across a car park, fully laden with her shopping. Through sign language, I asked her if this was the correct road into the city and the ferry terminal. With that, she bade me to follow her. This was easier said than done because I had to lift my fully-laden bike up and over a crash barrier before I could follow her. We crossed the car park and entered a small office where she introduced me to a gentleman and then promptly left us. The gentleman then took me outside and confirmed I was on the correct one.

As much as I was grateful to the both of them, I was aware that time was ticking and, because of my indecision, I was doubtful that I would be in time to catch the ferry for this particular crossing. With this in mind, I speeded up and, within a few hundred metres, this huge bridge came into view. It's amazing how such a large object could remain hidden until the very last moment. After crossing it, I knew I had to turn right and follow the side of the estuary towards the ferry terminal, but with so many traffic lights to negotiate, I, to my shame, jumped several red lights in an effort to be on time. The one good thing about Google street maps is that you have a very good idea of what the area looks like. So, after turning many corners, I knew straight away that I had reached the ferry booking office.

Now, because Japanese timing is world-famous for being to the second, I wasn't confident that I was in time to catch the ferry. So, after a flying dismount, I ran into the booking office just as the booking officer was about to change the scheduled sailing time. He gestured to the sign and I confirmed with a breathless "Hai" that I indeed wanted to use this sailing. With that, he started to take my fee as well as alerting the ferry of my late arrival. Not only did he do this, he even ran out of the office and stood in the middle of the road to stop any traffic, so I would have a clear run across the road and down to the waiting ferry. I cycled up the tailgate as fast as I could while at the same time trying to bow at the smiling ferry staff. No doubt, they were very eager to make up the 60 seconds lost while waiting for me. Having said all that, I was very grateful to them all for making sure that the ferry didn't go without me.

After a very enjoyable two-hour crossing to the island of Shikoku (I have to admit that I slept most of the way), I disembarked and made my way along the harbour and headed for the city centre of Tokoshima. I located my pre-booked hotel without any problems and checked in. Later, I enquired at reception about an evening meal. I was told that, seeing as it was a Saturday, the local restaurants might be fully booked, but to try anyway.

The excitement for me as a solo traveller is the thrill of trying to communicate with little or no knowledge of the language. However, in Japan, it is very different. While all the buildings were recognisable, their signage was indecipherable, giving no clue as to the purpose of that building. OK, a glass-fronted showroom with shiny new cars all lined up will give a bit of a clue as to its function, but most of the time it was just a case of sticking your head through the hanging curtain of any door which you thought might be a restaurant, or bar and hoping for the best. I proved to be correct about one said building when I stuck my head through the door. However, a young waitress waved her finger and pointed to her wristwatch, informing me that they were not yet open, and suggested that I come back in half an hour. After taking this opportunity to wander around the darkening streets for half an hour, I returned and was ushered to a row of stools in front of a kitchen counter and shown a pictorial menu presented on a smartphone.

Now, I'm a fish lover, so when a picture of a Caesar salad with salmon came up, I chose that. Then they asked me if I wanted sashimi salmon. I have to admit that I didn't know that sashimi was, in fact, raw salmon, but I still said, 'Hai.' Anyway, when it came, it was delicious.

Sitting there, it was obvious that I stood out like a sore thumb, a point of curiosity to the local people eating there. Fortunately for me, some of the younger diners knew a few words of English, so I was able to tell them that I had flown in from Manchester and was cycling across Shikoku – which seemed to impress them. Confusingly, though, after finishing my meal, I was presented with another meal, which turned out to be a pilgrim's meal. I was given this because the island of Shikoku is famous for its 88 Shinto shrines and many of the eateries give a free meal to pilgrims (known as Henro) who traditionally walk the 1207km route visiting these shrines. Despite not wearing the traditional white tunic, conical hat and carrying the wooden staff like most of these pilgrims would wear and use, I was still accepted as a modern pilgrim and, as such, in their eyes, warranted a free meal.

After finishing these meals, I left the restaurant, intending to go back to my hotel for an early night. However, my curiosity got the better of me and seeing that I had emerged unscathed from my first cultural soiree, I couldn't see any reason for not continuing in the same vein. My confidence was high and my curiosity piqued. I was on a roll and, with my newly found courage, I stepped out into the brightly lit streets on a mission to track down some night life. It was either by luck, or judgement, when I managed to find some traditional Japanese bars, where most of the diners and drinkers were ensconced behind curtained booths. So I quietly sat down close to the exit and slowly sipped my beer.

As I headed back towards my hotel, feeling somewhat pleased with myself on how the evening had gone, I noticed a dark, covered stairway leading up from the pavement, with a large neon sign at the top spelling out the word "BAR". Now, for some strange reason, this was an immediate attraction to me and seeing that the evening had gone so well, I thought that this would be the ideal last watering hole before retiring for the night. Since arriving in Japan, not once had I felt threatened; in fact Japan is one of the safest countries to visit. So, with that in mind, I climbed the dimly lit stairs, which led to a narrow modern bar. Inside, I found it was occupied by four young gentlemen. I approached the bar and, to my amazement, could see that they sold draft Guinness – one of my favourite drinks. So, with a cold beer in my hand, I took in my surroundings.

It wasn't long before one of the young gentlemen started asking me some basic questions, e.g., where do I come from and why was I here. So, I defaulted to using the required sign language and gestures, which hopefully informed him that I had flown in from Manchester that morning and I was cycling across Shikoku. Now, being a passionate Welshman, I had to tell him that although I had flown in from Manchester, I was, in fact Welsh and with that he produced his smartphone with a Welsh translation app on it. He then proceeded to have all his questions translated from Japanese into Welsh. How cool was that! In all fairness, his limited command of the English language was more than enough for both of us to have a decent conversation. After a little while, he informed me that his wife was learning English and could I have a conversation with her on his phone. So, I gave her my best "watashinonamaeha garesu jōnzudesu" (my name is Gareth Jones) and then proceeded to speak very slowly in English, informing her of my plans. How much she understood, I couldn't say, but I thought, *how surreal was that!*

By now, the evening was drawing to a close, so I said my goodbyes and walked back to my hotel. In my room, I went through the information given to me earlier by the receptionist. When I had arrived that afternoon, I had asked her if she could book accommodation for the next two nights, which would be situated somewhere high in the mountains. I had found it easy to book hotels in Japanese cities, but to book accommodation in remote mountain areas had proved impossible for me. So, I gave her the rough location of the villages I wanted to stay at and within 20 minutes, she had booked me in with two local guest houses. I was so grateful for this because if I had failed to secure accommodation for these two nights, then I would have to resort to using my small tent to wild camp somewhere in the mountains and I wasn't really looking forward to that experience, because all I had was a small tent and nothing else.

Leaving Tokoshima the following morning, the road slowly meandered its way up the wide-bottomed valley, skirting around verdant paddy fields and quiet, deserted villages. This 80km route into the mountains would eventually take me to the village of Minokoshi. Unfortunately, that Sunday morning, I had made a big mistake when choosing miso soup as part of my breakfast. Although it was very tasty, it was also very salty and for the rest of the day, I had to stop at every vending machine to quench my thirst.

Now, mobile phones have never been important to me, but I was advised by my family to purchase one. However, I did not have a Japanese mains adapter, so I called in at a shop which I thought may sell them, but however hard I tried to explain through sign language and gestures, I was not able to make myself understood. So I vowed not to use my phone unnecessarily – which suited me.

As the day wore on, the roads and valley got narrower as I approached the bottom of the mountains. It was at this point that a policeman stopped me. He did not speak any English, but during my years of learning karate, I knew that the word "sensei" meant teacher, so I confirmed this. I also informed him that I was heading for Minokoshi. He intimated that it was a long way and the road was steep and, with that nugget of information given, he got back into his car and drove off. It wasn't long before I met this policeman again. Fair play to him; this time he gave me a bottle of water to drink before driving off. As I continued further along the road, thinking it would be the last time I would see him, I discovered that he hadn't finished with me yet. Further up the road, he stopped to give me a map of the area, again very kind of him, but completely useless to me, because everything was printed in Japanese characters. The last time I saw him was when I was approaching a fork in the road and he was there to make sure I took the correct road. What a gentleman.

As I made my way slowly up the valley, I came across what I thought was one of those 88 Shinto shrines, nestling amongst the trees a few metres from the edge of the road. It was a solidly built wooden structure. It had a quiet, serene feel about and I'm glad I stopped for a while.

At the end of the valley, the road pitched up quite severely and I had to use my lowest gear in order to continue cycling. This road looked similar to the roads around my home, so I felt at ease, but the next few hours of continuous zig-zagging my way up this mountain really sapped all of my strength and I had to revert to walking on several occasions. By now, many hours had passed. I looked at my watch and it showed 17:30. At this point, not knowing how far I had travelled, or what distance I still had to cover, I was starting to feel anxious. Although it was a well-tarmacked road, there had been relatively few vehicles using it, so I was a little surprised to see a small white van coming down the road to meet me. I was even more surprised when he stopped opposite me. He wound the window down and said something. Obviously, I didn't have a clue as to what he was saying, but I did manage to catch the word Minokoshi. I hoped that it was the name of the village I was staying in for the night, so I nodded and said, 'Hai.' He then turned his van around and gestured for me to put my bike and belongings into it. Whether this was a wise move or a foolish one was yet to be established. I surmised that it would be very unlucky of me to accept a lift from a mass murderer and seeing that Japan is one of the safest countries to visit, I thought I'd take my chance.

Sitting in complete silence, he seemed friendly enough as we drove back up the mountain. After a couple of kilometres, I was starting to be curious as to where this village could be situated. There was no indication of civilization anywhere, just trees and the approaching top of the mountain. All of a sudden, we turned right into what seemed like solid rock. Just like a scene from a James Bond film, I half-expected to see a part of the rock face hinge open to reveal a megalomaniac's hidden stronghold, but all we did was enter a short tunnel, which conveyed us to the other side of the mountain and into the small hamlet of Minokoshi. I was relieved to discover that the driver was, in fact, the proprietor of the guesthouse where I was staying for the night. He had obviously been concerned with the distance I had to travel and the time it was taking me. So, I was very surprised but more than happy when he had decided to come and look for me.

Reading more about Japanese accommodation, I can only assume that his house, which was part of a shop, was a Minshuku-style of accommodation. It turns out that many Japanese families rent out unused bedrooms in a B&B-type of lodging. Regardless of the style of accommodation I was staying at, I was more than chuffed with the traditional Japanese meal that was given to me that evening. Amongst other things, it consisted of cold fish, cold pickled vegetables, tofu and hot rice. Mind you, I have to admit that I didn't eat everything on my plate (which would have annoyed my late father immensely), but, nevertheless, I was still very grateful for this authentic, traditional meal. Thankfully, I didn't come across like a complete idiot when using the chopsticks to tuck into my evening meal. That night, I slept on a futon bed laid out on tatami mats and had a very good night's sleep.

The following morning, while saying goodbye to my host outside his house, I noticed that there was a small shrine opposite, so I thought it courteous to run up to it and offer my thanks for such a genuine experience and then I set off in the rain down the side of the mountain away from the hilltop village heading another 80km to the small town of Motoyama. This route took me through many small villages and communities clinging to the very steep wooded sides and I was humbled by the helpfulness and warmth shown to me by everyone I came across. This included a female petrol station proprietor who, after confirming that I was on the correct road, gave me a hot can of coffee from their vending machine so that I could warm up a little.

One thing I noticed on the descent that seemed a little strange to me was the number of small lifelike scarecrows propped up on the side of the road. I learned later that a local woman from the Nagoro village made them. I'm not sure if she had made these particular ones, because I hadn't cycled through that village, but maybe someone was trying to emulate her skills.

I eventually arrived at Motoyama. I knew from my maps that the guesthouse was situated on the main street, but which one? Seeing as I had no idea, I enquired at a small office and the young lady, after looking at my written confirmation, indicated that the guesthouse was on the left further down the street. Unfortunately for me, even while cycling slowly down the street, I still had no idea as to which house it was. Thankfully, I heard shouting behind me and I turned to find the same young lady running up to me in the rain to show me exactly which house it was. In fact, she knocked on the door and introduced me to the proprietor. What an angel!

To my joy, this guesthouse seemed to be Ryokan-style. It had everything that I had hoped for. The ancient wooden structure was topped with the famous curved roof. Other traditional features included sliding doors and tatami mats, but reassuringly with a modern shower room, Western-style toilets and an internal hot bath called an onsen. After checking in, my female host could see that I was wet through and cold from the heavy rain so she showed me the room where the onsen was situated. She intimated that I must first have a shower before immersing myself up to my neck in the very hot water. Utter bliss.

Later that evening, she knocked on my door to inform me that my evening meal was ready. I gestured to her to see whether the T-shirt and shorts I was wearing were suitable attire. After looking me up and down, she went to a rail and produced a kimono and heavier overgarment for me to wear. She demonstrated how I should put it on correctly and then quickly left the room. After donning this authentic garment, I thought I looked like a noble samurai warrior. All I needed was a katana (samurai sword) and I would really look the part. However, my bubble was quickly burst when I entered the dining area. It turned out that everyone else in the room was wearing western clothing and did not give me a second glance as they watched their early evening programmes on the flatscreen TV. I felt somewhat conspicuous as I tried to sit cross-legged at the low dining table to eat another traditional evening meal.

By now, I'm sure you know that I like the occasional drink and when I thought I heard the name for beer mentioned at the start of the meal, I optimistically asked for bīru. Unsurprisingly, I was given an emphatic "ie", which sounds like "yeah", but actually means "no" – somewhat confusing, don't you think!

Although feeling tired from my day's exertion, sleep was slow in coming that night. This was due to the continuous croaking outside my window by what I can only assume were numerous amphibians enjoying a midnight chorus. Eventually they lulled me into a deep restful sleep.

The following morning, I had several options to take to the coastal city of Saijo. After gesturing to my male host, he indicated that although the scenic route around the local reservoir had a steep climb to start with, it would be preferable to cycling on the busy main road.

Although I had been 100% certain that my accommodation in the mountains had been booked for me, I wasn't confident that I would be able to locate them, so I had kept my one-man tent with me just in case. But seeing as I had pre-booked hotels from now on, I thought there was no need for me to carry it any longer, so I offered it to my host. I'm not sure if he understood me, or whether it is still leaning up against the wall of my room. Most probably he binned it as soon as I left.

After cycling alongside the beautiful tree-lined reservoir, I passed through a very long dark tunnel before joining the main road down to Saijo. Cycling through the many tunnels en route was fine, because in many cases, there would be an elevated pedestrian walkway keeping you away from the traffic, but this particular one only had a verge on which to cycle and I must admit that I felt relieved when I exited unscathed into the bright sunlight.

Cycling down from the mountains felt strange to me. It seemed that every deeply-wooded valley fell down into another deeply-wooded valley. As soon as you felt sure that you had arrived at the bottom of one, it immediately became the top of the next. Eventually, this rollercoaster of a road did bottom out and I arrived mid-afternoon in the city of Saijo and easily located my hotel.

Later on, I found a modern restaurant, which served a more recognisable plate of food. Up till this point, some elements of the traditional Japanese food given to me were an acquired taste, so at times I stupidly starting to fantasise about a simple plate of beans on toast. It was while at this restaurant, I had a lovely innocent encounter with a local girl. She had come in with her boyfriend and had to walk past me in order to reach her table. As usual, I stood out like a sore thumb – again a point of curiosity. She walked past me with a small grin on her face. This grin widened as she came past me again to collect cutlery. The third time produced a lovely smile and when they both finished their meal and exited, she turned around and gave me an even bigger smile and a wave of her hand. Not a word was spoken but, nevertheless, it was a lovely moment.

From Saijo, the only way you can cycle off the island and to the large town of Onomichi, is to head further up the coast to the city of Imabari and the start of the famous Shimanami Kaido bikeway. This bikeway takes you over six large bridges, linking six small islands and keeping you well away from the main expressway, thus guaranteeing a leisurely trip around those islands of outstanding natural beauty. Now, if I had known that the continuous blue line that now accompanied me along the edge of the road was in fact a guide for cyclists to follow, it would have been very easy for me to navigate around these islands. I just thought that, like our own white and yellow lines, this blue line was just a different colour to demarcate the edge of the road. Never mind, I took it as a lesson – a lesson which thankfully forced me to slow down and savour more of my beautiful surroundings.

I arrived in Onomichi mid-afternoon and took the ferry across the slow-moving river. Confusingly, my town map showed the river, but didn't indicate where the ferry crossing was situated. So, when I disembarked, I didn't know whether to turn left or right. So I turned right, hoping that something would miraculously appear to indicate where I was. Annoyingly, after 100 metres, I still didn't know where I was, so I approached a gentleman to ask for directions. I had learned the Japanese phrase for "can you help me" and humbly presented my map. He seemed to understand my predicament and quickly indicated on the map my precise location. It turned out I should have turned left but no matter; I retraced my steps.

I knew my guesthouse was situated along a long, narrow street but, to my surprise, this street turned out to be fully covered with a glass roof, very reminiscent of a long, glass-roofed market hall. Numerous shops, cafes and restaurants lined each side of it. It seemed strange to be in a covered area and still have to watch out for passing vehicles. Nevertheless, it had a lovely old-world charm about it.

After checking in, I dismantled my bike, thankful of the fact that I had experienced, without any breakdowns, many aspects of Japanese culture from the saddle of my trusty steed. Luckily, my Japanese hosts were a young couple who had lived in Australia for a couple of years. As a consequence, their command of the English language was good, which totally eliminated the need for awkward gestures and sign language on my part.

Later that evening, I went to a Japanese/Spanish restaurant further on down the street. It was busy, with many people enjoying a relaxing meal and drinks. My meal consisted of thinly sliced rare beef on a bed of salad leaves, complemented by several glasses of red wine. Again, I was drawn into conversation with some of the younger diners, which resulted in a very convivial atmosphere. Strangely, seeing that this restaurant had a dual culinary theme, Spain really wasn't represented that well. The only recognisable reference to the country was when the proprietor would, with a flamboyant gesture, shout '"adiós" to his departing guests.

On my return to my accommodation, my host asked if I wanted to go out with him to the local bars with some of his mates. It sounded fantastic but, to tell you the truth, I had consumed several glass of red wine earlier in the evening and I didn't need any more alcohol so, regretfully, I declined. However, I did spend an enjoyable hour talking to his young wife about their experiences in Australia. She even opened a bottle of sake for me to sample but, I have to admit, as a lover of single malt whisky, its subtle flavour was lost on me.

That night, I had the whole of the dormitory floor to myself, as no other guests had booked in – therefore a very peaceful night's sleep was guaranteed.

The following morning, I carried my bike bag and all my belongings slowly to the local train station and purchased a ticket to travel around the bay of Osaka and back to my starting place of Izumisano. The helpful stationmaster, along with his English-speaking colleague were apologetic when they informed me that I would have to change at four stations along the way. Luckily, good signage and helpfully painted footprints on the platforms helped me to navigate around any problems. At one station, I asked a guard for directions to platform 7. He, however, refused to answer me until he had completed his task of giving semaphore-style instructions to the train driver. He then politely indicated that platform 7 was at a lower level. By now, my last train was due to come in, so half-dragging and half-stumbling down the wide staircase, I landed on the platform, just as the train pulled in – phew, what a relief!

One memorable leg of this journey was a ride on the high-speed Shinkansen, commonly known as the bullet train. It was sleek, fast and oh so quiet – a fantastic experience, especially if you are only used to the clickety-clack of trains back home.

From my final station, I took a taxi to my last hotel. After checking in, I asked for the locations of various local eateries and, to my shame, I chose McDonald's. However, in the evening, I chose a modern Japanese restaurant to finish my memorable Japanese adventure.

The following morning, the hotel shuttle bus took me the short distance back over the water to Kansai Airport.

Thoughts on the plane

This was a trip which ticked all the boxes. When you choose a certain country to visit, it's usually because there is something that you particularly want to see or experience. Japan is one of those countries. I was so grateful to have experienced so many of the iconic and unique aspects of this fascinating country. I would have been pleased to see or experience just one of them. As it turned out, I stayed in an amazing, traditional wooden house and ate several traditional meals (OK, some of the items on the plate had an acquired taste but, nevertheless, still an experience). Luckily, I found I could use chopsticks without any real problems. Another highlight was relaxing in one of their famous onsen hot baths, plus I got to ride on the world-famous bullet train.

Although Japan is unique, one aspect of everyday life is very recognisable – they drive on the left like the UK, so stationary or approaching vehicles were a familiar sight – cars looked normal to me. No offence intended to countries that drive on the right!

In hindsight, I wish I had taken up the offer from my Onomichi landlord to go with him and his mates for drinks – I'm sure a cultural experience was missed.

I'm not sure if I saw any of the famous 88 Shinto temples. There were 20 in the Tokoshima area alone and I could have visited some of them if I had the time. Nevertheless, I did see a wooden structure and several small shrines on the side of the road, which, although may not have been any of the 88, were all equally thought-provoking.

While researching my route across Shikoku, one area grabbed my attention and that was the scenic Iya Valley. I knew that I would be passing close to it and really wanted to see the famous Kazurabashi vine bridges that cross over the Iya River. It's stated that some were built about a thousand years ago. Sadly, only three now remain intact. Regretfully, through my eagerness to cover the required daily kilometres, plus the already stunning vistas, I must have cycled past it without knowing and it wasn't until relaxing a few days later that I realised my oversight.

All the people I met were extremely helpful and courteous. When a Japanese person says yes, then you know that it will be completed on time and to a high standard. I'm sure you will never hear a Japanese person saying, "oh sorry, mate, I forgot", or "sorry I ran out of time". It's refreshing to know when they say yes, it means yes.

It's a country I will to return to, so if you fancy the idea, why not beat me to it and book a flight now – you won't regret it. Sayōnara.

The Second Prettiest Chunk – 2014

Carrick-a-Rede rope bridge

Now, I'm sure that many of you think that I'm quite selfish to cycle solo to all these different countries. Many people have asked me why Sue doesn't come with me. Well, the easy answer is that she wouldn't enjoy all that cycling and then living for a week out of her one and only piece of hand luggage. If it was a supported tour where all of her luggage would be transported to a decent hotel at the end of the day, then maybe she would consider it. I know she's more than happy to wave me off for a week or ten days, even if I do spend some of my nights in a decent hotel. So long as there is a bar nearby, she knows where I'll be. Nevertheless, knowing I have all this freedom to do what I want can only satisfy me so much. Having cycled in all these different countries and seen some fantastic sights, you really do need someone to share it with and, as a consequence, I cannot wait to get back and tell Sue all about my experiences and then bore everyone else with my intrepid tales of so-called adventures. No doubt, it would be a hollow experience if you couldn't offload the unforgettable sights, some hardships, and all those memories.

Yet, the thought of experiencing a cycle trip together appealed to me. So, with this in mind, a short trip around the North Antrim coast in Northern Ireland looked to be a suitable and enjoyable first trip together. And if things didn't turn out for the best, then it would be a relatively short distance home. I have read that it rates second only to the tip of the Dingle Peninsula as the prettiest chunk of coastal Ireland. So, we were on to a winner from the start.

Although Sue cycles 3.5km a day to work, I knew that cycling up to 15 times that amount would be unrealistic for her. So I had to scale down my expectations for this particular trip. So, one evening I tentatively approached Sue (a bit like a male praying mantis would approach a female) and casually enquired if she was up for a cycling trip together. She made it plain that it certainly wasn't her idea of a luxury holiday, but after thinking about it, she asked me to put a bit more meat on this particular bone, e.g., how many days, how many km per day and what type of accommodation would be available. I told her that there would be five days cycling with no more than approximately 40km per day and we would be staying in B&B accommodation. I told her that most people can easily cycle 16kph and if we break the amount of daily kilometres down into manageable distances and treat it more like a sightseeing trip, then the days should simply fly by. This information seemed to be acceptable to Sue, with the proviso that we wouldn't be extending the daily distances beyond what was promised and so I started making arrangements.

Booking accommodation in Larne, Cushendall, Bushmills and Limavady was relatively easy, but what is not that easy is the safe parking of the car. I wasn't comfortable with just leaving the car in a Belfast multi-storey car park for five days, so I looked for alternatives. Eventually, I found an ideal solution online where you could – for a nominal fee – legally park on someone's drive. It was in a prime location in the centre of Belfast and quickly allayed any fears I had about securing safe parking. After booking up all the accommodation and parking, all we had to do was look forward to a brilliant cycling holiday together. I was so confident about this trip that I didn't even suggest that Sue increase her daily millage in preparation for it.

At last, the very early morning arrived and we drove the 214km to the port of Holyhead on the island of Anglesey. The crossing to the port of Dublin was uneventful and we were soon on the M1 heading for Belfast. It's strange being on the road so early. You automatically think that it is later than it truly is. Annoyingly, shops are not open when you think that they should be – surely they know that we are passing through and make a special effort to open up for us! By now, we were both very hungry and more than ready for a full Irish breakfast. Luckily, one of the motorway service stations was opening up for such a feast and we pulled in. After thoroughly sating ourselves, we continued up the beautiful east side of Ireland.

After a fantastic view-filled drive, we crossed seamlessly into Northern Ireland, with the impressive granite mountain range of Mourne on our right to keep us company. Eventually, we turned off the Belfast ring road and slowly made our way into the centre of this famous city. Finding our off road parking was easy and I was soon pushing the doorbell of a newly built house. Despite no one answering the door, I confidently drove up to the top of the drive and we started unloading the bikes and our one and only pieces of hand luggage each. As we busied ourselves with this, a gentleman in a string vest came out from the side door. It was obvious that he had been in the land of nod and no doubt was none too pleased being woken from his slumber at this ungodly hour of 9am. He confirmed that we had the correct address and it was OK to leave our car there, or at least I hoped that's what he said, because it's quite difficult to tune your ear to the distinctive intonation pattern of the Northern Irish accent.

With our limited possessions attached to our bikes, we were soon heading for the River Lagan, which winds its way through the city centre where at its mouth it enters the Belfast Lough – an intertidal sea inlet connecting Belfast to the Irish Sea.

It was a nice gradual start for Sue as we slowly followed the river. We wound our way through wide boardwalks and pedestrianized areas, gradually making our way in a northerly direction through the city centre. At one point we could see to our right, beyond the river, Samson and Goliath, the two great yellow-painted gantry cranes of the Harland and Wolff dry dock. Despite the urge to stop and gaze at their structure and size, we were eager to push on and, before we knew it, we were cycling along the 40km coastal road on our way to the town of Larne.

At this point, I was more than aware that Sue would start feeling fatigued quicker than me. So, at every opportunity I would point to various landmarks, beautiful vistas, or points of interest, anything to distract her attention from her growing discomfort. At one point, as we cycled through County Antrim's oldest town of Carrickfergus, we saw a gymnasium on the second floor of a building. There, behind large plates of double-glazing, several people were frantically peddling on their exercise bikes. No doubt every one of them pleased with the amount of mileage their computers were showing. I know that any kind of exercise is beneficial and I applaud anyone who gets off their backsides to make the effort. Yet, I felt sad to see that they seemed to be quite content to remain glued to a bike going nowhere. Surely it's better for those who have an addiction for endorphin-releasing exercise to get out into the fresh air, instead of breathing in droplets of stale body odour oozing from various pores. As we cycled past, I enthusiastically gestured to them to be like us and drink in the beautiful Northern Irish coastline.

As mid-day approached, we stopped for a leisurely lunch overlooking one of the greens on a local golf course. As an accompaniment to our meal, we amused ourselves by observing the many different emotions that the golfers displayed as they approached the green. Some exhibited overwhelming joy from their approach play, others showed occasional anger, but mainly it was just the usual frustrations as they eventually holed out.

Back on the palm-tree-lined road again, the expanse of Larne Lough came into view. This gave us both a tantalizing view of the stunning North Antrim coastline we would cycle along after departing the following morning. For now, it was just what we wanted as we entered the coastal town of Larne.

Up till now, there were no indications of the troubles that had gripped Northern Ireland in the past. But, as we cycled around a roundabout close to the harbour, we could see the highly fortified police station, with more cameras and spotlights than you would see at a Britney Spears concert. From there, it was easy to locate our guesthouse where we checked in and secured our bikes. By then it was mid-afternoon, so we walked the short distance into the centre of the town and found a nice pub to relax in and congratulate ourselves on a fantastic first day.

Later that evening, we had a very tasty meal upstairs in a restaurant, where the room was literally filled with the muscle-bulging bodies of the local bodybuilding club. I looked pretty puny compared to them. However, as a consolation, the look of disappointment on Sue's face brought a smile to my face when she realised that she was unable to stuff any of them in her one and only piece of hand luggage. We finished the night off with a few drinks in the nightclub below.

The following morning, we set off on the coastal road proper. The dramatic headlands and bays, with their raw elemental beauty, kept us captivated as we slowly made our way to the village of Glenarm where we had a light lunch.

Cushendall was our next destination. Unfortunately, the wind had increased, which meant that, for the next 20km, I had to take the lead in order to protect Sue. Although the stunning coastline tried its best to take our minds off the weather, I thought that the cosy interior of a pub in Waterfoot would be a suitable refuge and thankfully Sue agreed. Had we known that Cushendall was only another three kilometres away, we would have pushed on, but this was a welcome break from the relentless wind and an ideal chance to chat with the friendly locals.

Arriving in the pretty village of Cushendall, we sought our accommodation for the night. It was easy to find, because it was a large Georgian townhouse on the main street. Alarmingly, though, there was a note on the door requesting guests to contact the number displayed. At the time, our mobile phone was quite basic and I thought that I may have missed an important message from the landlord. So we tentatively dialled the number, thinking that we may have to search elsewhere for accommodation. Thankfully, the landlord answered and told us that he would come straight away. Within two minutes he arrived and informed us that we would be the only guests in the building and that we could choose any room we wanted.

After selecting an appropriate room, I suggested that we could wander around the village and maybe call in some of the pubs we saw coming in but, understandably, all that Sue wanted was to lie on the bed and go to sleep. So, I went to a couple of pubs and chatted with some of the older drinkers, relaying the details of our cycling trip.

In the evening, we had a very good meal in a restaurant just a few doors down from our B&B and finished off the night by having a drink in a lovely old pub opposite. This building was a real blast from the past. It felt like you were entering some kind of museum, depicting life from around the turn of the twentieth century. Inside, the small room had the atmosphere of a back parlour, where the focal point was situated around a green AGA cooker and most of the chairs were of the old-fashioned small Windsor-style – hard! Despite this, it had a lovely, homely feel about it, with countless pictures and photographs adorning the walls. The locals were more than willing to regale us with local tales and gossip. We told this one particular gentleman (who turned out to be a retired policeman) that we had stayed in Larne the previous night. This led him to warn us that some people around that area were not very friendly, but I have to admit that his view was far from the truth. In our experience everyone was very open and accommodating, and more than willing to engage us in conversation. No doubt it is very naïve of me to hope that, despite people's religion, history and politics, it would be good if everyone just got on with each other.

Returning across the street to our accommodation, it was a bit spooky entering such a large empty house, but we soon settled down to a well-earned night's sleep.

The following morning, we awoke to the sound of someone downstairs busying themselves with chores. We thought, *fantastic, maybe that person is preparing our breakfast!* But when we came downstairs, we frightened the life out of this woman, who clearly had no idea that there were guests staying. After finishing off a hastily prepared breakfast, we were soon off on what turned out to be quite an epic leg on our sightseeing trip.

From Cushendall, the A2 gradually made its way up through the Glens Area of Outstanding Natural Beauty. Low hills and wooded valleys framed well-kept farms on the way up onto the side of the bleak and windswept Knocklayde moorland.

After a fairly windswept and tiring 24km, we arrived at the small seaside town of Ballycastle. We had a comfortable lunch overlooking the quaint harbour and the small island of Rathlin, but I knew that we couldn't stay long, because we wanted to see the Carrick-a-Rede rope bridge and the Giant's Causeway before arriving at our accommodation in Bushmills. Luckily for us, the rope bridge was only 9km away via the coastal road, but we still had to negotiate the very steep road out of town. This was far too steep for Sue and she had to push her bike most of the way up it. However, we soon arrived at the car park leading to the famous bridge. To access it, you first have to walk approximately 0.8km along the coast. Apparently, this impressive bridge was first erected by fishermen more than 250 years ago to catch Atlantic salmon. Now, it's just a tourist attraction. Nevertheless, it's still quite scary as you walk over the bridge suspended 30m above the rocks and crashing waves below.

By now, it was mid-afternoon and we still had to cycle another 14km to the World Heritage Site of the Giant's Causeway. Now, some of you may be counting up the kilometres and have come to the conclusion that this has now exceeded the daily amount of kilometres I had promised Sue. I have to admit that I truly thought that I had calculated the correct distances prior to the trip, but evidently my calculations were wrong, but, like a true gentleman, I didn't tell Sue this.

When we arrived at the main entrance, we were told that, because we had cycled there, admission was free, so we secured our bikes and walked the 0.8km along to this natural phenomenon. It's still baffling to me how volcanic fissure eruptions can result in such precise interlocking hexagonal basalt columns. Anyway, after marvelling at this incredible feat of nature and taking the obligatory photographs, we made our way back to our bikes.

Luckily for Sue, our accommodation was only 4km away and although I thought that an extra 10km on top of the 40km I had promised was not too much to add on, she was really tired. Retrospectively, one thing I didn't take into account was the extra distances we had to walk that day. However small these were, it still all added up to a tiring day for Sue.

We were relieved to discover that our accommodation was a lovely large, modern bungalow on the outskirts of the distillery village of Bushmills. After checking in, Sue lay on the bed, exhausted after her day's excursions and went immediately to sleep. Heroically, I forced myself to walk the short distance into the village to find a suitable restaurant for our evening meal. While I was there, I thought it would be remiss of me not to spend the next hour or so checking out the local pubs on the main street. It was only after returning, that I finally succumbed to the day's fatigue and had a quiet snooze to recover!

Later that evening, after returning from our meal, we heard the distinctive booming and ratatatat of drumming coming from a recreational area. We assumed that it was practice for the marching season. It certainly woke us up.

The following morning, we turned away from the coast and headed inland to the large town of Coleraine. It was along this stretch that Sue picked up our one and only puncture. Luckily, it was the front wheel, which allowed Sue a little respite from cycling as I mended it. After fitting a new inner tube, we entered Coleraine and made the decision to head back to the coast, hoping it would be a little quieter, so we re-joined the A2.

Seeing it was close to midday, the road sign for the seaside village of Castlerock persuaded us to try and find a nice café to have lunch at. The straight road down to the village was a pleasant freewheel and we soon covered the 0.8km and found a café next to the railway crossing. However, after the meal, the joy of cycling back up to the main road quickly turned into a sweat-inducing crawl and thoughts of, *why did we chose this*, kept flitting through our minds.

Continuing on the A2, we once again freewheeled down into the aptly named hamlet of Downhill and as we approached the bottom, the stunning 11km expanse of the Benone Strand beach opened up in front of us. Apparently, it is the longest beach in Northern Ireland and very popular with tourists and surf lovers. We both thought that it was certainly comparable with any exotic destination in the world and it's right on our doorstep. But, knowing we still had another 22km to our accommodation in Limavady, we reluctantly turned our back on this Northern Irish jewel and pressed on with the climb up and away from the beach.

From this point on, the low mountain range of Binevenagh came into view. With vertical cliffs and a flat top, it felt like a smaller version of the famous South African Table Mountain of Cape Town. To admire these beautiful vistas further, we stopped for an ice cream. Unfortunately, the ice cream and stunning views did little to reduce the fatigue which Sue was again starting to experience. To further compound her growing discomfort, she realised that, due to my previous miscalculations, there was a strong possibility that she would again have to cycle a greater distance than she had been promised. Unfortunately for Sue, this was indeed the case and we had to endure yet another unplanned day of cycling 50km before we could arrive at our accommodation on the outskirts of the market town of Limavady.

We were relieved to discover that our accommodation was another lovely large modern bungalow, situated down a long straight drive across large open fields. Again, after checking in, Sue sought the comfort of our bed and promptly fell asleep. I, true to form, cycled the short distance into town to look for a suitable restaurant for our evening meal (well, that was my excuse anyway!).

Later that evening, the thought of cycling into Limavady had lost its appeal for Sue and so it was suggested that it would be better to walk into town. It made a pleasant change and, despite Sue's lingering fatigue, we soon covered the 2.5km into the town centre. After eating in a lovely modern restaurant, we moved next door to a quaint old Irish pub, where it still retained the original floor plan of small snug-like rooms and open fires. To celebrate our journey so far, we toasted ourselves with a glass of whiskey in front of a lovely warm coal fire. At this point, the landlord was very generous and emptied the remaining amount of whiskey from the bottle into our glasses, which made us even more relaxed and happy.

Feeling warm and cosy, we decided to make our way back to our accommodation. This time, we didn't retrace our steps, but continued along the street and down onto the bypass. This was further to walk but, as we were both feeling refreshed, the extra distance didn't seem to bother us. Maybe Sue was starting to recover faster from the day's excursions than previous evenings?

The next day was to be our last day of cycling and, this time, we took a more direct route to Northern Ireland's second largest city of Derry/Londonderry. Although we were still on the A2, the traffic had started to increase and when, after 14km, it morphed into a duel carriageway, it made us feel very vulnerable cycling so close to heavy traffic. The close proximity of the City of Derry Airport didn't help with the volume of traffic, so I advised Sue to keep close to the inner edge of the wide road verge in order to reduce the pulling effect created by the speed of passing lorries. This strategy didn't really reduce Sue's anxiety, but I didn't have any detailed maps of the area in order for us to take a safer route. So, I took the pragmatic approach and told her that if she was going to fall, then to fall to her left – away from any vehicles. I can't repeat what Sue said that I could do with that suggestion, but eventually, after enduring this hair-raising 14km, we entered this famous city.

Regretfully, we didn't have enough time to explore the city properly, because we were taking the train back to Belfast. So, our priority was fully concentrated on finding the station and securing tickets for ourselves and our bikes. Luckily, while waiting for our train, we could see the iconic s-shaped structure of the Peace Bridge, which spans the River Foyle. Apparently, it was built to improve connectivity and convey pedestrians and cyclists between the two sections of the city and is described as a "structural handshake".

As with all things, our time had quickly come to depart, but our trip was far from over, because the next leg has been described as "one of the most beautiful rail journeys in the world".

As our train pulled slowly out of the city, it followed the River Foyle out to the wide estuary with its mudflats and headed into the lush green countryside. Before long we had arrived at the golden sands of Benone Strand, the same one which we had admired the previous day. This time the railway track ran alongside the sand, so we had a spectacular view of one of the most unspoilt beaches in Ireland. From Castlerock our train ride continued along the banks of the River Bann before sweeping into Coleraine. From there, the journey left the coast and headed inland. I have to admit that we both had a little snooze before eventually pulling into the Belfast. I wouldn't describe the first part of our train journey from Derry as "one of the most beautiful rail journeys in the world" but it certainly had some lovely views, with an excellent perspective of the coastline running along the beach.

After locating our car, it crossed my mind to spend some quality time in Belfast, but we didn't really have enough time, so we drove out of the city and headed south to the Republic of Ireland port town of Drogheda, where we had booked B&B accommodation. Worryingly, when we knocked on the door of this large house, the gentleman declared no knowledge of our booking. Luckily for us, I produced a printed copy of our booking confirmation with him. With that, he invited us in and showed us a room. At this point it was clear that this room had not been prepared for us. Even the en suite had to be cleaned by Sue before she felt that it was suitable to use.

Later, even the walk into town had a depressing feel about it. One pub we called in had CCTV cameras everywhere, which made us feel uncomfortable, so we quickly finished our drinks and made our way back to our accommodation. Thankfully, our meal at an Italian restaurant was very nice.

The following morning, when we came down stairs, the proprietor asked us what we would like for breakfast, but we informed him that we were leaving due to the fact that our bedroom was below our acceptable standard. Fair play to the man, he did apologise and waived the booking fee. However, it was a disappointing end to what was a fantastic trip.

Thoughts in the car

Despite having initial reservations about our Northern Ireland trip, we were more than happy with the outcome. Everything about it was positive and we couldn't be happier with the warm welcome we received from everyone.

Watching the decades of troubles relayed on what seemed to be nightly occurrences, Northern Ireland at the time seemed to me a dark and dangerous place to live let alone visit, but, in reality, it was stunning. Certain names and areas conjured up images of hatred and fear, yet when we passed by, there were no hints of its troubled past. I know that this is a sweeping statement and I'm sure that many people will say that my simplistic view of the troubles is too naïve and that I have no right to an opinion. Yet, I can't help thinking that, despite all the hurdles that Northern Ireland has to cross – and maybe it's a bridge too far – I just hope that everyone concerned will take a deep breath and continue talking, because I believe that this beautiful country has too much to offer to just let it regress back into darkness.

I know Sue was apprehensive about the amount of daily kilometres she had to cycle, but in all fairness, despite of my miscalculations, she didn't complain too much. It's a trip that both of us remember with fondness.

If you want to visit a place overflowing with spectacular scenery, which is not too far away, with ancient history and more than a warm welcome, then we wholeheartedly recommend Northern Ireland.

Enter the Red Dragon – 2015

Tian Tan Buddha

Ever since I watched the famous 1973 karate film, *Enter the Dragon*, featuring Bruce Lee, I have been fascinated with Hong Kong. In my teenage mind, it seemed to me an exotic place, with the very names of Lantau, Kowloon and the New Territories, conjuring up images of excitement, intrigue and danger. At the time, any thoughts of the transfer of sovereignty over Hong Kong to the People's Republic of China in 1997 seemed to me many years into the future and something I need not dwell on – doesn't time fly! We all know that you shouldn't judge a country on the strength of a film. I just hoped that all these years later, I would at least experience a bustling, vibrant city with a multicultural balance of both worlds. A fusing together of the best of East and West – and I couldn't wait.

Frustratingly, the fulfilment of this dream was put into jeopardy at the first hurdle. When I presented my passport at the check-in desk at Manchester Airport, the check-in clerk could not help but notice the poor condition of my passport. She enquired as to the reason why it was so poor. I told her that it got wet the previous year while cycling in Japan. She agreed that the crumpled and smudged pages could have been a result of the wet conditions, but it did not account for the delamination of the clear plastic veneer covering my photograph. She demonstrated this delamination by sliding her thumb nail up under a corner of it. I asked her politely not to exacerbate the situation and tried to convince her that I was a genuine traveller and not some illegal immigrant. Unfortunately, my explanations fell on deaf ears and she promptly informed a senior member of staff who quickly took my passport off for closer inspection. There followed an agonising 20-minute wait outside an office. Sitting there, I didn't know if I would be allowed to keep my passport or, indeed, continue my journey. Dark thoughts of being arrested for possessing a fake passport raced through my mind. Fortunately, the Dragon Gods were with me and the gentleman informed me that I would be able to continue through check-in. He did, however, suggest that, on my return, I renew my passport as soon as possible. Relived, I returned to the check-in counter and asked the lady who had dealt with me previously to write a note confirming that they had checked my passport and found it to be genuine, just in case the airport authorities in Hong Kong questioned the validity of it. She, however, declined my request, explaining that they were happy with my explanation, but could not guarantee that Hong Kong authorities would accept it. So, for the entire flight over, I was fearful that I could be refused entry and all the implications which come with that scenario.

After an uneventful 13-hour fight, we touched down on the manmade island of Chek Lap Kok and taxied up to the beautiful, modern international airport of Hong Kong. I tried to keep as calm as I could as I made my way through immigration and offered my passport to the officer. It was a tense moment, but I was more than delighted when he accepted it without question and I passed through.

After this ordeal, I was a very relieved and happy person as the early Sunday morning sunshine poured through the large windows of the arrivals lounge. Holding on tightly to my one and only piece of hand luggage, I searched for transport details.

Standing in the middle of the arrivals lounge, I enquired at the information desk as to the best method of dealing with transport issues. They advised me to purchase a reusable contactless stored value smart card called an Octopus card. This would make my life a lot easier when dealing with MTR (Mass Transit Railway) and other modes of transport. I then read the bus timetables close to the exit of the airport. They gave all the information needed to transfer me to Hong Kong Island and my destination of Wan Chai. As you can imagine, the bus timetable gave information on countless journeys and their times throughout the week. So, after careful study, I realised that the time most suitable allowed me to nip back to the arrivals lounge and have a cup of tea. It was during this interlude that this thought occurred to me: instead of going straight to Wan Chai and having to wait for the availability of my hotel room, this would be an ideal time to visit the world-famous Tian Tan Buddha. Apparently, it is one the biggest seated bronze Buddhas in the world and seeing as

I was quite close to it, it would be daft not to make the trip this morning – after all, it was on my to-do list.

After finishing my black tea, I went back to the information desk. They informed me that the cheapest mode of transport was to take the bus from Tung Chung to Tai O. From there, take a second bus to Ngong Ping. I could then walk to the big Buddha. They said it would be the easiest, but I thought it sounded quite difficult. Alternatively, I could pay for a taxi, or get the shuttle bus from the airport to Tung Chung and ride on the longest cable car system in Asia. Seeing as I had never been on one, the cable car sounded quite exciting, so I took the gently sloping corridor leading to the exit of the airport. This gradually introduced me to the unaccustomed humidity waiting for me outside. Beads of sweat started to roll down my face as I jumped on the shuttle bus taking me over the bridge from the airport to the new satellite town of Tung Chung.

After alighting from the shuttle bus, I envisaged having a difficult time trying to locate the cable car station, but in the end it turned out to be very simple. I just headed for a building with a great big cable car system sticking out of the side of it. I entered the complex and climbed the stairs to the booking office. Luckily, I was more or less the first person in the queue, so I didn't have much time to decide which type of gondola I wanted to travel on. In all fairness, it didn't take me long to decide that, although it was more expensive, I opted for the glass bottom one.

So, after queuing for a short time with four young Asian students, we climbed into our gently swaying gondola and started on the 5.7km journey to Ngong Ping. To start with, everything was fine because the cable car system was still quite close to the ground, but it soon started to climb steeply away from the station and up over the muddy waters of Tung Chung

Bay. It was a little disconcerting looking down through the glass bottom at the water below, but the look on the faces of the students and their efforts of trying to keep their feet on the gondola frame and not on the glass brought a smile to my face. Despite their unease, We were soon over the bay and quickly climbing up the steep, wooded hillside. It was at this point that the mist came down. It completely obliterated any view that we had had and I was starting to worry that the Buddha may also be covered in mist, but, thankfully, as we approached the top of the hill, we were able to glimpse him in the distance.

After alighting at Ngong Ping, I was confronted by a very modern village. Almost like a film set, it was very clean and obviously catering for the thousands of tourists who visit everyday. I read that it was supposed to be a culturally themed village, but I have to admit that I was a little underwhelmed by it.

After making my way past the obligatory retail outlets, eateries and souvenir shops, I came to an impressive arch signalling the start of the Po Lin Monastery area, and the huge Buddha. From this point on, the impressive Buddha completely dominated the top of the hill, especially now the mist had completely disappeared. This awesome structure was constructed at the start of 1990 and took three years to build. It stands at 34m high and weighing over 250 tons.

Now, to get up close and personal to view his smiling face, a total of 268 daunting steps had to be negotiated. As I mentioned before, even at this time in the morning, the humidity was quite high and therefore many people were resting on the climb up and down. Anyway, I reached the top without any problems and breathed in the views. There, I discovered that this imposing bronze statue was in fact sitting on a lotus flower surrounded by six other smaller statutes, which represent meditation, wisdom, generosity, zeal, patience, and morality. Access to all of this was free, but I paid a small charge to go inside the hollow Buddha and the exhibition hall, where, amongst other things, I viewed a relic of Gautama Buddha.

After absorbing as much enlightenment as I thought safe, I decided to return via the cable car, where, for some meteorological reason unbeknown to me, we were again surrounded by a thick mist. It was slightly eerie to hear ghostly voices so close to you emanating from this wall of white before being relieved to find that it was only the excited voices of people in the opposite gondola passing us. Halfway down the mountain, the mist handed us gently back into the sunshine, with impressive 360-degree panoramic views over the airport and Lantau Island.

After emerging from the station, I noticed several bus stops with information posted to lamp posts. So I quickly found my stop and waited. While waiting at Tung Chung, I couldn't help but think of the thousands of people who lived in the high-rise buildings in front of me. These great big concrete monoliths completely dominated the area. Every one of them was identical to the next. I know that it is a home for many thousands of people, but it made me very grateful and aware of how lucky I am, having been brought up on a small farm and consequently living in detached dwellings since. I couldn't really imagine being cooped up so close to other people.

The bus dutifully arrived and after confirming my destination with the driver, I settled down to the relatively short journey on the North Lantau Highway to Hong Kong Island. This highway hugs the coastline for 20km before crossing over the Kap Shui Mun Bridge and then on to the impressive Tsing Ma Bridge. From there it crosses Tsing Yi and on to Kowloon. From there it goes through a tunnel and emerges onto Hong Kong Island.

I knew from maps that Hong Kong Island was kidney-shaped and that Wan Chai was in the middle of the inner curve. So I knew I wasn't far from my destination and so moved closer to the front of the bus. Fair play to the driver, he noticed me and stated that the next stop was Wan Chai.

After alighting, I was once again subjected to the oppressive heat, humidity and my first encounter of the hustle and bustle of Wan Chai. I knew that the hotel, Gloucester Luk Kwok, would be close by, and if I had walked a little further down the street, then I would have found it at my first attempt, but I didn't, so it took me an extra 10 minutes to locate it. Relieved, I checked in and a porter took me to the 21st floor, and opened the door to a large, spacious room overlooking the main street.

After unpacking, I found myself outside and pinned to the hotel wall, thinking how I could get away from these crowds and the oppressive humidity. I have to admit that my first thought was to see if there was a bar close by and, sure enough, I discovered a small air-conditioned one in the narrow street behind the hotel. It was run by Filipino girls with large posters of musicians covering the walls – I felt at home.

That evening, I was hungry and took a stroll down the brightly lit streets. A gentleman standing outside a doorway obviously thought that I was a man desperate for an evening meal and suggested that I choose his restaurant. However, for some unknown reason, I graciously declined and walked on. It didn't take me long to stop and ask myself why I had refused. The place looked clean and tidy, with many people eating there, so I turned back and went inside. The proprietor and staff took good care of me, serving a tasty seafood platter. All of this was washed down with a little too much wine, but I struggled through it. Luckily, this restaurant was only around the corner from my hotel, so I was soon in bed fast asleep.

The next morning I went for a walk and found myself ogling a Lamborghini Aventador in a car showroom and a Ferrari parked at the back of the hotel – I quickly added them both to my imaginary "to-have" list.

Seeing that Guinness is one of my favourite drinks, I was soon attracted to a large Irish bar. However, my joy was short lived, because this black liquid posing as Guinness tasted completely different and a world away from the black nectar brewed at St James' gate in Dublin.

That evening, holding on tightly to my newly found confidence, I went to a Thai restaurant. Again I had a tasty fish meal and a few drinks to finish. Unfortunately, the following morning, the Delhi belly's Chinese cousin paid me a visit, which took up most of the morning's activities. I can only assume that jetlag and the migraine during my flight were the reasons why I stayed in bed until midday listening to the rain pounding on my window.

Hong Kong is a fascinating place to visit, with many must-see attractions. So that afternoon I went exploring, trying to familiarise myself with my surroundings. It is so easy to use the MTR system and I soon found myself in Kowloon. I wanted to visit the Jade Market and Temple Street night market and wanted to make sure that I knew how to get there and get back in the dark.

Temple Street itself was obviously deserted this time in the afternoon, apart from a young lady who suggested that I to go upstairs to view her impressive jade collection. It was a very kind offer and I thanked her, but quickly moved on.

The Jade Market itself is a low wooden building situated underneath a flyover and is home to many stalls. After perusing the building, I bought some nice jade pendants to take home. I then walked back down Temple Street and back to the MTR station.

That evening, I returned to the popular Temple Street night market. Despite the many watches, pirated CDs and DVDs, plus fake label clothing, sports and everyday footwear, nothing really appealed to me. So, as I left the crowded street, I couldn't help but think about the young lady who, only a few hours previously, had wanted me to view her impressive jade collection. I'm sure with the amount of people now in the street, she would have more than enough viewings.

The following morning I read about the Peak Tram. This funicular railway carries both tourists and residents from the Central District to Victoria Peak. The steep track covers a distance of about 1.4 kilometres, with an elevation of 396m. It has a maximum steepness of 48% with a track gradient of 4-27 degrees.

To access the Peak Tram's lower terminus, I had to walk the 1.7km from my hotel, passing impressive-looking office buildings before joining a long queue for a tram ticket. Once aboard, I sat down on smooth, well-worn wooden seats for the five-minute journey up to the peak. On a clear day, it provides stunning views over the famous Hong Kong skyline, harbour and beyond. Unfortunately, the mist from Lantau Island must have taken a shine to me, because when I reached the top and eagerly ran over to the viewing point – guess what, I couldn't see a thing. I'm sure that the mist is put on just for you to temper your disappointment by buying items from the many outlets around the viewing area. Needless to say, they didn't secure their foreign holiday on the amount of money I spent there, because I just turned around and returned the way I came.

Obviously, all my trips have to involve some amount of cycling. Initially, I thought I could spend days cycling all over the area, but, after careful research, I soon realised that unless you travel out into the New Territories away from the

Metropolis, Hong Kong is not the easiest or safest place to cycle around. Having said that, this particular cycling box still had to be ticked and, as you know, "fortune favours the brave". With this in mind, I had researched suitable cycle hire shops on the island and had located one further along the bay on Kam Ping Street. So, I decided that the next day would be the day I would find this shop and tackle this humidity full on from the sticky saddle of a push bike.

The next morning, I jumped on the MTR to North Point. Exiting from the station, I turned right and started my search for Kam Ping Street. I walked 200m down the King's Road without success. I then crossed over and came back up the road opposite – still no success. I asked at various stores for directions, but no one seemed to know where Kam Ping Street was (perhaps it was too wet to camp!). Anyway, by now I was starting to worry that I may have to admit defeat and find another bar and drown my sorrows. However, one shopkeeper came to my rescue and told me it was situated on the other side of the street. Now, if I had turned left when exiting the station, then it would have been the first side street I would have come to (the choices you make in life!). Anyway, with my faith in humanity fully restored, I marched up to the shop only to discover it was closed and would not be opening until later in the day. So, I went back on the MTR and did something which was very easy on the wallet and that was some window shopping. I also avoided a banner-waving protest march.

Luckily, when I returned later, the cycle shop was indeed open. I told the proprietor that I wanted to hire a bike for the rest of the day. However, before he would give me the bike, he wanted to see my passport. Now, I was very reluctant to go back to my hotel to get it because it was now mid-afternoon and I wanted to complete the circumnavigation of Hong Kong island before it was too late. I'm not sure whether he didn't like to see a grown man cry, or the fact that I pleaded with him to take pity on me, but most probably it was when I offered to give him all my available money as a guarantee that finally made him relent and give me the bike. In all fairness, he was very helpful and showed me, on his computer, the roads I needed to cycle on in order to successfully complete my ride.

With a suitable helmet fitted, I was felt invincible and confidently cycled back down to the King's Road on the start of my 42km circumnavigation of Hong Kong Island. It was at this point when it quickly dawned on me, that there were no cycle paths to ride on – nothing but nose to tail traffic. Then, by some miracle, the traffic all stopped and I thought, *now's my chance* and took off like some scalded Peking duck, but I was soon engulfed by the many lorries, cars, buses and taxis – all of them trying to squeeze me off the road. I did try to get on the pavement, but in many cases it was encased by bamboo scaffolding and when there was a gap, there were too many people trying to squeeze me back onto the road. Luckily, for a few seconds, the traffic light system would predictably come to my rescue, reducing the volume of cycle-hungry traffic before engulfing me once again.

Thankfully, this ebb and flow of traffic allowed me to safely negotiate the busy headland of North Point, before branching off right onto the smaller road up to Chai Wan. From there, I turned right onto the far quieter Tai Tam Road, which wound its way through wooded valleys and passing the low-rise upmarket residences of Red Hill. At this point, the road started to hug the side of Turtle Cove, offering beautiful vistas of the calm sea and outlying islands. It wasn't long before I turned off this road and down to the popular seaside village of Stanley. Seeing as I didn't have the luxury of unlimited time, I didn't stay too long, only sampling a flavour of its unique vibe as I slowly made my way through its market stalls.

Cycling back up to the Tai Tam Road, I continued on around the southern part of the island. Within 4km, I had reached the expensive residential area of Repulse Bay. As to the origins of this English-named area, there are many stories which lay claim, but none with any conviction. As I couldn't offer an alternative, I just cycled on. I quickly turned off on to Island Road and on to the equally expensive residential area of Deep Water. Apparently, if you are a billionaire and you've a spare quid or two, then this is the place to live – I couldn't agree more.

By now, it was starting to become busier as I approached the town of Aberdeen. It is famous for, amongst other things, its floating seafood restaurants and the famous dragon boat race. The town is very popular with tourists who can access it easily by catching a bus and making the 29-minute journey. Another mode of transport – although more expensive – would be the ten-minute train journey from Admiralty. Although you may think that you are a long way from the central area of Hong Kong, in reality it is only two miles as the crow flies over the other side of the mountain.

Before I knew it, I had negotiated the southern part of the island and had worked my way around the mountain and started to make my way back into the bedlam that is Hong Kong. Keeping to the smaller streets, I slowly made my way back into Wan Chai.

Needing to return my bike, it suddenly dawned on me that I had travelled to North Point by the MTR and I wasn't sure how to get there by bicycle. Anyway, I knew I couldn't go too far wrong if I kept the sea to my left. However, after cycling through Victoria Park, I thought it would be better for me to ask a local. So I entered a shop, confident that this person would know how far North Point was. Frustratingly, this woman didn't know. She even phoned up someone and they didn't know either. It turned out that it was only 50m up the road. This makes you realise that, when you are lost in a strange country, you can't always rely on local knowledge.

I delivered the bike, along with the sticky saddle, back safely to the shop and having been reimbursed with my guarantee money, jumped back on the MTR for well-earned R&R.

By now a pattern was emerging. During the morning I would try to see some of the many attractions on offer. At night I would find a restaurant and then a bar and have a couple of drinks. Now, seeing as I'm a part-time musician, I try to find the pubs/clubs offering entertainment. One of the clubs was the famous Joe Bananas (others are available!). It had a relaxed atmosphere, with good live music.

I felt very safe walking around Wan Chai at night, with many families still evident. However, the closer it came to midnight, the less confident I felt. I found that, after this time, you became easy prey for the madams who wanted you to use their facilities.

One aspect of walking the streets at different times is the difference between the more familiar sights of the day, compared to the neon lit streets of the night. During the day, each street reverberates with the diverse sounds of commerce, while at night, those same streets hum to a different tune. It's hard to orientate yourself. Was this the same street I walked down the previous evening? All signs of the mundane commercial enterprises had totally disappeared, morphing into a festival of lights, each one eager to befriend the willing and enthusiastic revellers.

Talking about easy prey, I thought I would again visit the shopping and entertainment district of Kowloon. However, after exiting the MTR station, I was immediately set upon by touts handing out leaflets urging me to buy a tailor-made suit. Confronted with these very determined people, I quickly pushed past them, thankful of the fact they didn't pursue me down the road. Besides, I wouldn't be able to fit one of them into my one and only piece of hand luggage anyway.

Having quickly moved on down Nathan Road, I soon became bored with the choice of shop windows I was able to peer through. It seems that the same type of shops, e.g. fashion, gold, jewellery, sports and computing, were replicated every 100m and therefore I thought it was quite pointless to continue. So I decided to run the gauntlet back to the waterfront and take a return journey across the bay on the famous Star Ferry. I have read that a poll of travel writers had at one time rated it first in the "Top 10 Most Exciting Ferry Rides". I thought, *wow, this must be good*, and so eagerly stepped on board. I'm not sure as to the extent of their excitement, because if you like sitting on wooden seats listening to diesel engines and breathing in diesel fumes on the 10-minute journey across Victoria Harbour, then you would be in heaven, but for me it was just OK. Having said that, I'm sure there are many different ferry routes conveying you around the sights and sounds of Hong Kong, which would rapidly ramp up your excitement levels!

On the penultimate day, I tried to think of an attraction that I had missed. You could spend many holidays exploring everything Hong Kong and the surrounding areas have to offer. But when you have ticked the boxes of the must-see attractions, e.g. the Buddha, Temple Street Market, Jade Market, Peak Tram, Star Ferries, Stanley, Aberdeen, and the stunning coastline, I was struggling to think of one where I could just pop in and have a look. So I just went for a walk down the narrow streets of Wan Chai and to my joy discovered a traditional Chinese street market. It turned out that this interesting attraction is one of the biggest outdoor street markets found on the island and sells a wide range of goods, which attracts both tourists and locals alike.

It was while I was perusing the street that I stopped at one of the many jade stalls, and, seeing as I still needed to buy a souvenir to take home, I cast my gaze over some of the many bangles for sale. I had read that the vast majority of wares sold at these stalls were either imitation, or of low quality jade, but I was just looking for a cheap and attractive trinket. So, I tried, as recommended, to negotiate the price down. Unfortunately, my haggling skills were rubbish and I knew I had paid far too much for it. So, to take my mind off my embarrassingly easy capitulation, I wandered on further up the street.

After passing many food and live fish stalls, I finally entered an internal market area. Finding nothing that I wanted buy that could fit into my one and only piece of hand luggage, I found myself on the other side of the market on Queen's Road. This was an area which I hadn't explored, so I continued on down the street. Leaving the Wan Chai area, where most of the buildings are high-rise, Queen's Road was a little more open and the reason soon became apparent when I found myself standing outside Hong Kong's Happy Valley Racecourse.

Now, seeing as I'm not a gambler, it didn't occur to me that horseracing is the most popular sport in Hong Kong. In fact, it can boast of two racecourses. This particular one was first built in 1845 on swampland. Apparently, at the time, it was the only piece of flat ground suitable for horseracing, and as a consequence, it soon pampered to the horseracing desires of the British people living there.

Racing at Happy Valley usually take place on Wednesday nights and is open to the public as well as members of the club. The racecourse and stands are capable of accommodating approximately 55,000 punters. If you are unable to buy a ticket, then you can take a trip to the New Territories and the impressive Sha Tin Racecourse where it boasts an even bigger capacity of 85,000.

I didn't want to seem nosy, but standing outside of this huge facade, my curiosity got the better of me, so I started walking down and through a covered entrance next to the Jockey Club. Unbelievably, I soon found myself standing on the side of the racecourse. I nervously looked around and then quickly ducked under the rails and walked a few paces on the actual course itself. It felt very daring and I expected someone to come along and escort me out – but today, I was the only one there.

My time in Hong Kong was fast coming to a close. My mind was full of the exciting things I had seen. Sadly, it's one thing to travel and see these exotic places, but if you haven't got friends and family to tell, then you only bring home an empty feeling. So, I couldn't wait to get back and tell everyone.

One frustrating element of flying is your departure time. If your flight is around midday, then you can vacate your room and more or less go straight to the airport. Unfortunately for me, my flight wasn't due until 23:00. That left me in a quandary; do I try to find another attraction, or just walk around aimlessly for 10 hours? I solved this problem by partly doing a bit of window shopping, then sitting on the promenade watching the ferries come and go – basically people-watching. This strategy saw me while away the hours in a leisurely manner.

As dusk approached, I suddenly realised that I hadn't seen any of the famous Hong Kong junk boats. There were many of them in the film, so I definitely wanted to see at least one. And one is all I did see. Despite being a very common sight in the 60s and 70s, there is now only one authentic junk boat moored in Victoria Harbour. The *Duk Ling*, built in around 1955, is primarily used for sightseeing tours of the harbour. So, to get a closer view, I walked to the end of one of the piers and quickly took a picture of it before the light was too low. As I turned to walk away, I felt it looked a little sad and lonely, the last boatman standing at a nautical party – the token relic of a bygone age.

By now it was almost dark and although my one and only piece of hand luggage wasn't that heavy, after many hours of carrying it around, my shoulders – like some Hong Kong residents – were protesting. Luckily, to take my mind off it, the famous Symphony of Lights came to my rescue. It is a multimedia event, featuring a spectacular lighting display synchronized to orchestral music. Dancing laser beams shoot from the roofs of many buildings on each side of Victoria Harbour. Whole sides of buildings light up in a large dazzling display of movement and colour.

As I walked along the promenade on my way to Central and the MTR station, I came across an advertising film crew. Two young attractive models were standing on a large cylindrical platform, posing as a newly married couple. Various spotlights were angled on their faces to try to catch this very romantic moment. With the iconic backdrop of the Central District fully lit up, then, who was I to argue.

This trip certainly lived up to my expectations and as I travelled on the relatively quiet, high-speed train back to the airport, my mind kept racing with all the sights and sounds of this vibrant, if a little daunting country.

Thoughts on the plane

Having fulfilled the dream of exploring Hong Kong, I felt a little disappointed and deflated as the aeroplane rose up and away. We all know of the characteristic symptoms you feel at the end of a holiday. Those pangs of regret of not fully experiencing local history and culture. Yet hadn't I seen all of the sights that were listed as "must-do" and "must-see"?

With many of my cycling trips consisting of me cycling a linear route from one area, or town, to another, here in Hong Kong, I had an ideal opportunity to fully immerse myself in its unique sights and sounds, yet I still found myself stupidly rushing past them, declaring, 'been there, got the T-shirt.' To be truthful, I didn't really know what to expect. Perhaps it was me just ticking a box and not allowing myself to see beyond.

Hopefully, next time, I will take my time and open my eyes before ticking a particular box. Perhaps it was me trying to experience too much of the film I had seen when I was 17 – who knows?

Even if you hate martial art films, why don't you fly out and visit this unique place and experience it all for yourselves.

Iceland Delivery – 2016

Hallgrímskirkja Tower

As a change to my usual choice of destinations, the Nordic country of Iceland had a certain appeal. Famously known as the "Land of Fire and Ice", it offers a plethora of natural wonders, with many volcanoes and glaciers just waiting to be explored – so I thought I would take a closer look.

I knew in the time available, it would be unrealistic for me circumnavigate the 1322km ring road, yet I still wanted to experience its stark, dramatic landscape for myself. Let's face it, who wouldn't want to explore Iceland, even a little bit of it. So, I decided to fly into Keflavik International Airport and spend a week in the capital, Reykjavik, and hopefully hire a bike for a day and see what the city and surrounding area had to offer. At the time there wasn't a direct flight from Manchester into

Keflavik, so I had to fly into Germany and then get a connecting flight from there.

Nothing really prepares you for the bleak Icelandic landscape. As we approached Keflavik, it seemed to me that it was a grey and colourless place, more like the surface of the moon than a vibrant modern country. After going through the usual control procedures, I found myself outside the small airport and wondering, which was the best and cheapest method of making my way to the capital.

Usually, I try to keep the cost down as much as possible by looking for the best deal. However, when people heard of my plans, they warned me that it is a very expensive country to visit and I would have to dig a lot deeper into my wallet for even the smallest item. So, instead of spending a lot of fruitless time trying to see if I could find some cheap transport to take me from the airport, I just took a deep breath and walked up to the nearest bus displaying the name of the capital and climbed aboard. The driver asked me where I wanted to be dropped me off. After explaining where my accommodation was situated, he explained that he could drop me off fairly close to it, but I would then have to walk the remainder. I settled down on the 45km journey, alternating the view of the sea to my left and a flat, barren, treeless landscape to my right. In the distance was a low range of hills punctuated by what I can only assume to be small extinct volcanoes.

As we approached the small seaside town of Hafnarfjordur, the bus stopped outside a Viking-themed hotel. Although it had been given some characteristics of a wooden Nordic hall, with faux dragon and serpent finials fixed high upon steeply pitched gables, it only hinted at its ancient proud lineage and most probably was far removed from a proper Viking longhouse – yet I'm sure it appeals to the many tourists who stay there.

After a few more stops, I was dropped off close to my hotel. Within a few minutes, I had checked into what seemed to be part-hotel and part-Chinese restaurant. My first-floor room was small, but adequate.

By now it is late afternoon, so I went exploring. My accommodation was situated at one end of the main street, which terminated after 1km at the lower level before the start of the Old West Side district. Pleasingly to the wallet, I noticed that many of the bars and pubs had happy hours at different times. So, to make the most of the cheaper prices, it made sense to me to remember the sequence in which they appeared as not to double back on myself.

Later that evening I found a restaurant with a fairly reasonably priced menu and after calling in on a few bars, made my way back to my hotel. No doubt, it's quite obvious that I enjoy having two or three beers and generally I'm in complete control of myself and my actions. However, on this particular evening, either due to jetlag, or most probably underestimating the strength of the local beer, it transpired that, when I went to my room, I must have fallen very quickly asleep, because the next thing I remember was waking up halfway down the stairs leading to the basement and the restaurant's kitchen area. Luckily, I was still fully clothed and made a hasty retreat back up to reception. I remember that the previous bar had toilets downstairs, so I can only assume that I thought I was still in that bar trying to access them. With a foolish grin on my face, I went back to my room only to discover that I had locked myself out. By now, I was fully awake and with an even bigger grin on my face went back down to reception and asked the manager for a master key to access my room – a lesson learned.

The next day was filled with a greater depth of exploration of this lovely city. Any window shopping was followed by a sharp intake of breath at the high prices displayed.

The following day, after much searching, I eventually located a cycle hire shop at the harbour in the Old West Side district. There, one of the staff told me of a 30km cycle ride around the perimeter of the city extending out and beyond the suburbs. Seeing as I couldn't realistically cycle beyond the city limits, this short distance would have to be enough to appease the Nordic cycling gods and just adequate enough for me to tick the "I've cycled in Iceland" box. With my cycling integrity just about intact, a basic map of this route was given to me and I set off.

It was a very pleasant ride and apart from getting lost once, it gave me an intimate understanding of the geology of the area. Many ancient lava boulders, having eventually solidified enough to stop their slow menacing advance, created a meandering path for me to follow. These large boulders graphically demonstrated the immense power that a volcano can generate. Thankfully, they have lain unmoveable for centuries. Yet, with approximately 30 active volcanos on the island, who's to say whether it all could so easily change? (this would certainly disrupt my happy hour schedule).

After returning the bike, I went to the local tourist information centre to have a look at what other adventure-type experiences were on offer. Trying not to make a comment on what I thought were astronomical prices for these trips, I chose the one I had seen on TV and that was snorkelling in the narrow rift between two tectonic plates. I know I'm not articulate enough to describe the sensation of floating above a huge crevice and I know it will be difficult to do justice to this natural wonder, but I'll try.

After being picked up the following morning by our British instructor, we drove the 52km through the desolate landscape to the Silfra fissure, which is one of the many fissures which had opened up during the earthquakes of 1789. As we approached the wide, flat, open Thingvellir valley, I started to get excited. It's not every day you get the chance to snorkel between two tectonic plates.

There was only one other person in the minibus with me and he was a Chinese interpreter who was equally excited as me. The rest of our group had made their own way to the site. So, when we alighted from the bus, we joined them, making a small group of approximately eight people.

From the small car park there was no obvious entry point, just a flat terrain punctuated by small black pools. So, after changing into our dry suits, we waited nervously for our instructor to secure our belongings in the back of the minibus and show us the way. It was at this time that several of us realised our big mistake of donning our dry suits *before* using the small portable toilet. No doubt, this daily occurrence brings a small smile to the faces of many of the instructors. Despite this small faux pas, we were soon ready and set off on foot to the entry point a short distance away. Again, it was very confusing. There was no obvious start, no banners stating the uniqueness of this natural wonder, just slow moving streams, like large rock pools meandering around on their slow journey to the nearby Þingvallavatn Lake, which apparently is the second largest lake in Iceland.

OK, we had some idea as to where the start was, because we had to wait for a group in front of us to swim away into one of those pools. So, as we approached the pool we noticed a galvanised steel platform built between two rocks. At this point the water was relatively shallow at roughly six-foot. It was shallow enough to see all the coins which had been tossed into the pristine water for good luck. I didn't think I needed to pay for good luck, seeing as I had paid enough for this adventure, so I just put all of my faith into our instructor being highly competent.

Eager to experience this unique adventure, I volunteered to be the first to climb down the short ladder on to the platform. After fitting my mask and snorkel, I was told to climb down another short ladder into the water, place my face into the water and start slowly swimming away from the platform. Even after been told of the high buoyancy of our dry suits, it takes a lot of courage to put all your faith into an item of clothing and push away from terra firma. The intense cold of the glacial melt water from the nearby Langjökull glacier immediately hit my face, literally taking my breath away. Then, suddenly, like a trap door opening, the floor beneath me fell away and I was suspended over the tectonic boundary between the North American and Eurasian plates. It was difficult to estimate the width of the crack at the surface. I would think that it was approximately eight metres. The depth was harder to estimate. It's stated that it is close to a 100m. All I know is that I couldn't touch the bottom.

It was a strange sensation with the water halfway up your face mask when looking up to see where you were drifting to. It showed a strange dual aspect, with the familiar world above the water and an oh so silent alien world below. Slowing drifting on this bed of pure clear water – reputed to be the clearest in the world – it certainly lures you into thinking that the objects far below are closer than you think.

By now, I was unaware of anyone around me. I was totally transfixed on the size of the boulders, which had fallen into the deep fissure during previous earthquakes. It seems their erratic journey to oblivion had been halted as they got wedged deep down where the crack narrowed. I couldn't even hazard a guess as to the size, or depth, of them. But for some primeval reason there was a strange magnetic pull, like something was calling me to come down and take a closer look! It's an eerie world down there with all shades of green, blue and grey, slowly diffusing into a shimmering blackness. Apparently you can scuba dive as well, but to dive to this depth is seldom done as it requires highly technical diving skills. After about 100m, the fissure finally closes up and reluctantly releases its hold on you and you swim somewhat ungainly into a shallow lagoon.

Climbing out onto terra firma, I waited for the rest of the group to emerge. It was at this point when I realised that our instructor was swimming on his back, his one arm cradling an American lady, who had apparently had a panic attack halfway through the swim. Ironically, she was a marine biologist, but this experience was obviously far too real for her. Also, my friend, the Chinese interpreter, failed to even start the swim, stating that he had aggravated an old injury after descending the ladder. All I can say is that they had missed out on a once-in-a-lifetime experience, to which they would surely regret.

After returning to our minibus, we changed back into our clothes and were then transported the short distance to the rift itself. As Iceland is situated on the Mid-Atlantic Ridge, the Thingvellir National Park is one of the only places on Earth where you can view the meeting of both the North American and Eurasian tectonic plates rising up from the ground to form a high cliff face. It's an awesome sight as you walk between the high walls of jagged rocks, with many boulders delicately balancing themselves on top, just waiting to come crashing down at the smallest tremor, or, heaven forbid, someone's loud sneeze. Rightly so, this natural phenomenon has been a UNESCO World Heritage Site since 2004. As well as a worldwide attraction, Thingvellir is also an important historical place. Apparently, in 930 CE, Icelandic chiefs and lawmakers established the first democratic parliament (Alþing) and gathered here every two years to determine the laws of the land.

After threading our way along a manmade path, we zigzagged our way up through the high walls and out to a hospitality building overlooking the rift. After an hour's break, we climbed back into our minibus, which had driven around to pick us up and travelled back to Reykjavik, still buzzing with excitement.

Later in the evening I decided to go to an American bar and nightclub to reward myself for having such a fantastic experience. I made sure that I had been standing at the bar at least five minutes before the happy hour expired. Unfortunately, it took more than five minutes to serve me. Finally, when the barman poured my drink, he asked for the full price. I immediately informed him that I had been waiting a long time to be served. Luckily for me, an American who was sitting on a stool next to me confirmed that I had indeed been waiting before the deadline, so the barman reluctantly charged me the cheaper price. It took a long time to drink that beer, mainly because of the excellent music being played by two musicians. I was so engrossed by their skill; I stayed listening to them until they finished at two o'clock in the morning.

Exiting the nightclub, I was expecting to walk back to my hotel in relative darkness. Yet, I emerged into a soft twilight, more like late afternoon. There I was feeling tired, but everywhere around me seemed to suggest that I should be starting a brand new day, instead of finishing off the old one— Certainly a strange surreal feeling.

I awoke in the morning to bright sunshine and made my way down to the restaurant for breakfast. Now, despite a Chinese meal being very tasty, occasionally the unique aroma can linger overnight and be a little off-putting in the morning, especially if you are a little delicate after a session the night before. But, I am pleased to say that I was always proved wrong. Every morning I was greeted to a fresh-smelling room, with no hint of the meals enjoyed the night before. As a consequence, I always tucked into a variety of tasty breakfast dishes.

Now, seeing that my wallet had taken quite a hammering the previous day and to prevent it from going into a complete meltdown, I chose the cheapest option I could think of and that was to explore the city in greater depth. I walked halfway along the main street and up an incline on the left to the magnificent Hallgrimskirkja (the church of Hallgrimur). At 74m tall, it is Iceland's tallest church and the country's sixth-tallest building overall. The front elevation looked, to me, like a large vertical version of the Space Shuttle ready to launch. Apparently, the architect was inspired by basalt lava flows, which creates a landscape with elegant sweeping steps. It's certainly an impressive building both inside and out and completely dominates the Reykjavik skyline.

After absorbing as much of its splendour as I could, I left the church to search for lunch. I headed for downtown Reykjavik, which is the historical and cultural heart. Vibrant and lively, the area is home to the majority of the city's bars and restaurants. There is a maze of small streets with the more traditional brightly coloured corrugated metal-clad buildings happily rubbing shoulders with larger modern buildings.

Now, I love fish, so the restaurant of the Fiskfélagid Fish Company was an instant attraction. Housed inside a former 19th century store, the ground floor restaurant was accessed by crossing over a small bridge, while the cellar restaurant was accessed via the sunken outdoor seating area under the bridge. I chose the cellar restaurant. Inside, the light from outside flowed through small windows built high in the stone walls, giving the room a very atmospheric feel about it.

After perusing the menu, the Arctic char took my fancy. Then, while sitting quietly, I regressed back to the meals we had as a farming family. All the meals had been large, with the bulk of them made up of potatoes and other vegetables and, if you were still hungry, then filling up on bread was the only solution. In fact, I'm sure there's a lot of people who still judge a meal by the size and not necessary by the taste. When the meal arrived, the urge to spread it around the plate, making it a larger-looking meal than it truly was, was strong. If it hadn't been for the basket of bread, together with different types of butter, the size of the meal would have been very disappointing. Yet, after slowly consuming it, I came to the conclusion that, despite its small size, it had been the best meal I had ever tasted. I can't recall every item on the plate, but I remember the combination of small balls of pickled apple and the fish was really a match to savour. One other surprise was the bottle of water supplied. I have never tasted water like it. It's stated that Iceland has exceptionally pure spring water, and I would certainly agree, especially as I had been told that Icelandic water can smell and taste of sulphur.

Walking around this touristy area after my meal, I thought it strange that it is also known as the government district, with the Russian, Canadian, Finish, French and Indian embassies in close proximity. I continued walking around and eventually found the Saga Museum. Inside were lifelike wax figures depicting Iceland's history. Indeed, they are so lifelike that if you look carefully at one of the figures, his chest moves up and down, making him spookily lifelike. Although it is a relatively small museum, the exhibits and audio recordings gives you a good, realistic understanding of Iceland's early beginnings.

On my return, I went back to the tourist office and booked a tour to the Leiðarendi Lava Cave for the following day.

The next morning I was picked up by another minibus and after collecting a gang of young enthusiastic lads and lassies from Yorkshire, we drove 25 minutes southwest to the lava field close to the Blue Mountains. Leiðarendi is in fact two caves, formed by two separate eruptions. During each eruption, rivers of lava slowly cooled from the outside as they travelled from their erupting craters. A hard rock shell formed over the molten liquid, and as this was flushed out, a hollow tube was left. In this case, the two caves collapsed into each other, leaving a circular path which you can walk, stoop and crawl through.

As we all alighted from the bus, it wasn't obvious where to go, but as we walked the 150m across the tundra, a large hole appeared in the ground where the hard rock shell had collapsed, exposing the lava tube. After scrambling down to the entrance, we entered and made our way slowly in the darkness with only our head torches showing us the way. At times you could easily stand upright during the 900m-long circular route. Other times you had to resort to stooping or even crawling. This was encouraged so as not to disturb the unique rock formations formed by nature during the 2000 years since the eruptions. Some on the ceiling looked like shiny sharks' teeth worn down over the years.

It didn't take that long to explore the cave fully and all too soon we were back out into the daylight. However, for some members of the group, this exploration was long enough. After scrambling around in a claustrophobic pitch-black environment, even for this short length of time, the bleak tundra was a welcome sight for them. For me, the lava tube gave an easy access into this cool mysterious subterranean underworld that surrounds the Reykjavik area and I thoroughly enjoyed the experience. By the way, the Leiðarendi caves, which translate to "the end of the journey" is so called because the carcass of a dead sheep was found at the end of one of the tunnels.

The next day, I headed for the harbour. The city grew up around it and in the early 20th century it became one of the centres of the Icelandic trawling industry. In recent years, tourism and whale watching have gradually replaced fishing vessels, while shops and restaurants have occupied most of the warehouses.

After admiring the moored ships and boats, I headed for the relaxing Tjörnin park and garden with its large lake. I learned later that if I had looked more closely, I could have visited the famous Icelandic Phallological Museum. The building contains the world's largest display of more than 200 penises and penile parts belonging to almost all the land and sea mammals which could be found in Iceland. I have to admit that it would have been a fascinating museum to visit but, in truth, with nothing really *standing out* to grab my attention, I must have just walked straight past it.

With two days to go, I booked up my last excursion, which was a circular trip to see the famous geyser and the Gullfoss Falls.

The following day, I was picked up by one more minibus. My fellow passengers were a chatty bunch and we happily exchanged our Icelandic experiences. En route we stopped at a service station for refreshments and souvenir shopping. One part of the floor had thick glass covering the remnants of a room which had succumbed to the forces of a previous earthquake. This graphically showed us what the forces of nature can easily do to manmade structures.

I can't recall the exact location, but we called in to see a low, wide waterfall, rumbling softly in front of us. Just before leaving it to continue our trip, our young guide and driver, resplendent in his thick, hand-knitted "lopi" sweater, gave us all a sliver of dried meat to eat. Again, I can't recall exactly what meat it was, but at least it wasn't a slice of hákarl the famous fermented shark.

Eventually, we arrived at the geyser geothermal area of Haukadalur. Strokkur and Geysir are the biggest geysers in the area, with Geysir itself giving us the word "geyser". It's very popular with tourists, because the smaller Strokkur is more dependable and can erupt to a height of up to 30m every 5 to 10 minutes, whereas the bigger Geysir rarely erupts now. There are also more than 40 other smaller hot springs and fumaroles nearby, which keeps everyone interested.

After taking the obligatory pictures of the erupting Strokkur, we quickly covered the 9km to the awesome Gullfoss Falls. It's stated that it is actually split into two falls. The upper waterfall has a drop of 11m, while the lower one has a drop of 21m, with a total cumulative height of 32m. The actual canyon walls on both sides reach heights of up to 70m. With this amount of water, it's not surprising that it's the roar that you hear first. When you walk down on the wide cinder track, it's the raw energy that takes your breath away. As with most water, there's a strong magnetic pull that implores you to get closer, to feed off its immense strength. It even makes you wonder what it would be like to jump on its back and hurtle down into the great all-consuming Gullfossgjúfur canyon.

To actually experience this natural rollercoaster ride up close and personal, you can walk out along a wide shelf to the top fall, which gives you the sensation of being in the middle of this raging torrent.

Simply glued at the edge of this awesome spectacle, it's not surprising that I got completely soaked from the continual spray being generated. As with most of the visitors, I was a sorry sight trudging back up the path to the café situated above the falls. I may have mentioned before that I don't enjoy getting my clothes wet, so no amount of overpriced souvenirs could make me feel any better. I just wandered aimlessly around the large shop and restaurant before eventually achieving an acceptable level of dampness. Despite this mild irritation, I had thoroughly enjoyed this awesome display of nature's strength and majesty.

On returning to the capital, I spent my last evening walking around this wonderful city having another tasty meal and a few drinks.

The next morning, I walked to the bus station and took one last look around before climbing on board for the return trip to the airport. Annoyingly, at the check-in desk, they informed everyone that they were unable to issue a boarding pass for the transfer flight at Frankfurt and suggested that we obtain one when we arrive at Germany. Now, it's all well and good saying that, because when arriving in the transfer area at Frankfurt airport, I didn't know where to obtain one. I was somewhat flustered because I knew that the transfer time was very tight, so I just headed for the nearest desk and asked them for one. With a roll of their eyes, they reluctantly printed one out and I ran out to the waiting bus to take us to the far and most probably cheapest end of the airport.

Sitting in this small aeroplane, I couldn't help but have a smile on my face. Despite my frustrations, this small irritation of boarding passes paled into insignificance when remembering my experiences in "the Land of Fire and Ice".

Thoughts on the plane

As with most countries, I am used to being surrounded by ancient geology. The majestic Cambrian Mountains are not too far away from where I live. Their noble peaks rising approximately 541 million years ago – give or take a year or two. Closer to home, the nearest thing we had to a volcano was the volcanic intrusion of dolerite, which formed the solitary, yet distinctive, Corndon Hill. So, to come to such a young country that is still evolving was certainly different to the dependable and familiar landscape of Mid Wales. With approximately 130 active and inactive volcanoes in Iceland, it's not a certainty that you would wake up each morning to the same familiar views of the previous day.

Although we have found many innovative methods of harnessing this force of nature, we all know that we can't control any of it. We are simply at its beck and call. We keep our fingers crossed that our destructive methods don't interfere too much with the steady rhythm of nature. I'm sure there are some mega rich and clever people frantically searching for a solution to prevent nature destroying our structured way of life. Yet, it only took a relatively small Icelandic eruption in April 2010 to cause enormous disruption to air travel across Western and Northern Europe. Luckily, at the time of my trip, the island was relatively benign and a joy to visit, with everyone more than happy to coexist with their potentially fiery neighbours.

Now, regardless of the high cost of living, if you are like me and drawn to stunning natural beauty, coupled with the chance of some unique adventures, please make Iceland your next trip. With sublime food and warm hospitality to savour, it is well worth visiting.

Looking for a Scottish Moose – 2017

Canadian moose

A few years ago, I was given a thought-provoking book titled *Fifty Places to Bike Before You Die*. It's a fascinating book to read – assuming you've still alive. It shares the many places in the world where its author and other cycling contributors have cycled in. As I've stated before, one of the main criteria for my cycle trips is the length of time I can dedicate to them. I cannot and will not spend more than ten days. It's not fair to Sue. So, after reading through the book, one trip stood out for me and that was completing the Cabot Trail, which comprises of a large loop of the island of Cape Breton in the Canadian Maritime province of Nova Scotia. It's stated to be named after the 15th century explorer, John Cabot, and at 298km long, it would take me five days to successfully circumnavigate it at an average of 70km per day. At its northernmost point, a part of this famous

Cabot Trail passes through the Cape Breton Highlands National Park and, as a consequence, is considered to be one of the world's most beautiful cycle rides. Apparently, the stunning Highland Park was established in the 1936. This was hoped to promote tourism and protect some of Canada's most famous mountains, forest wilderness, coastal beauty and charming fishing villages.

This particular trip seemed a little strange at first, because all of my trips had started in an easterly direction, but, for once, just like the early explorers, I couldn't wait to head out west. Closer to the date, I decided to explore the option of hiring a bike instead of taking my own bike with me. I had taken my bike with me on a several trips, but there's a lot of faffing about, especially when you have to dismantle it ready for transportation and then the length of time it takes to reassemble it at the other end. So, I decided to hire instead. I trawled the various sites on the internet and chose Pedal and Sea Adventures. They confirmed that they could deliver a suitable road bike and meet me at the international airport of Halifax and Stanfield.

The next thing on the list was to try and buy a return bus ticket to take me the 320km from the airport to Baddeck. This small village is situated on the shores of Bras D'Or Lake and is reported to be the start of the Cabot Trail. Although all the information was on their website, the bus company did not allow anyone to buy a ticket online, but instead insisted you contact them by phone. Now, this is very simple for most people, but due to my occasional stammer, I do not have the same amount of confidence which others seem to have while talking on the phone and I usually try to avoid it if I can. My other fear was whether I would be able to hear them, thinking naively that the reception would be poor. Anyway, one evening I took the plunge and contacted them and was very surprised and relieved to hear a very clear female Yorkshire accent – what luck! After giving me all the spiel about the trip, she casually stated that, due to re-routing, the bus didn't actually go to Baddeck, but bypassed it. The closest scheduled stop would be at Wagmatcook, which is 14km this side of Baddeck. Although this was a little annoying, I was happy enough to cycle this distance with the proviso that there would be enough daylight to cycle it safely. With that goal in mind, I duly paid for my tickets.

As usual, Manchester is the easiest airport for me to fly from, but there was no direct flight to Halifax, so I persuaded my daughter, Nia, and her husband, Richie, to drive me down to Heathrow so I could take a direct flight from there.

Now, the beauty of only having my one and only piece of hand luggage is that you can go through check-in and passport control very quickly and before I knew it, I was sitting down in the departure lounge having a cup of tea and looking forward to my Canadian adventure.

Eventually, after a pleasant flight, I arrived at the award-winning Halifax airport (which award they had actually received, I never did discover). I just hoped that my international arrangements would be OK, but thinking about all the things that could go wrong, I was feeling less than confident at this point. The arrangements with Pedal and Sea Adventures meant that I would have to wait at the airport's pickup point until I was contacted. Looking out through the terminal's long wall of glass, I wasn't exactly sure what to look out for. Conducting business over the internet with an unfamiliar company doesn't give you any indication of the size or capabilities of that company. Would they arrive in a new purpose-built white van, a sporty car pulling a trailer, or maybe a beat-up old truck? Thankfully, I didn't have to wait too long to find out, because a small car suddenly appeared outside, with a road bike strapped to a rear mounted cycle rack. My mounting anxiety quickly evaporated when they turned out to be a friendly young couple and it wasn't long before we had concluded the paper work and I was left alone.

Before making my way to the nearby bus terminal, I decided to return inside and confirm with the bus company's check-in desk that my bike would be accepted as stated on their web page. Worryingly, it took 20 minutes for that person to contact someone else to verify that I could indeed take my bike on the bus. When I had initially contacted the bus company, I was informed that I would have to place the bike into a clear polythene bag in order for the bus driver to place it safely in the hold. This bag would prevent the bike damaging or soiling other luggage placed close to it.

By now, it was mid-afternoon and knowing I would be facing at least a long four-hour journey up to Baddeck, my anxiety began to grow again. Despite making small talk with a woman who was waiting with me, I couldn't help but worry that it would be too dark to cycle. Eventually, this large modern coach drew up and, reassuringly, the driver placed my freshly wrapped bike into the hold.

After securing everything, we set off – albeit 30 minutes late. Yet, despite my growing fears, I settled back and contented myself by looking out at the countless number of coniferous trees lining the Trans-Canada Highway. I naively thought that it would be a straightforward 320km journey, but I was completely wrong. The coach quickly turned off the highway and made its way to a small town. There, it picked up and dropped off items at the bus depot. Passengers came and went, some noisy, some quite, all of them familiar with the ebb and flow of local life. Frustratingly for me, this was the theme throughout the journey. Every time the bus driver accelerated up to a decent speed, he would have to slow down again. Amongst all of this stopping and starting were the usual comfort breaks, which obviously extended the length of time this long journey took and sorely tested my patience. There were even university campuses to slowly negotiate.

By now, I had resigned myself to the fact that I wouldn't arrive at Wagmatcook during daytime hours. However, accepting this inevitability posed a big problem. When I had requested the bike company fit front and rear lights to the bike, they had only fitted small LED lights, the type that made you visible to other road users, but certainly not strong enough for you to safely navigate by. I had hoped that they would have been stronger for cycling along unfamiliar roads, but this wasn't the case. Staring out through the rain-streaked window into the black and wet evening, it was quite apparent that this busy highway was certainly not the place to cycle along, especially in the dark. So I had to come up with a plan B. The only viable alternative I could see would be to alight in Wagmatcook and hopefully find a taxi rank with a vehicle big enough to accommodate a plastic-covered bicycle.

Eventually, Wagmatcook emerged through the blackness. However, it was quickly evident that this stop was only a glorified petrol station and I would have to telephone for a taxi. Gratifyingly, I wasn't the only person on the coach who had problems with the bus not going to Baddeck. A young American cyclist also voiced his concern when we had stopped at Wagmatcook. To our relief, the bus driver, when hearing our dilemma, stated that the only thing he could do to help would be to stop at a petrol station on the Baddeck bypass and drop us off there. This was ideal, because it would be close to a turning for Baddeck and close enough for the young

American, who would only have to cycle a little way back down the highway to his own accommodation. With relief spread across our faces, the coach pulled away from Wagmatcook and, within 15 minutes, pulled into the large car park of this impromptu stop. Within five minutes the driver had unloaded our two bikes and after we expressed our sincere gratitude, he disappeared off into the night.

Due to the minimal amount of light coming from the nearby petrol station, it took another 15 minutes for me to unpack the bike, stash the polythene bag neatly away, and then attach my panniers to the bike frame. I then bid farewell to my young American friend and skipped across the wide highway. Reassuringly, it was only a short distance to cycle up to the junction and the small road leading to Baddeck. Having said that, my night vision was not yet good enough to gauge where the edge of this smaller road ended and the wide gravel verge began. As I suspected, the small LED front light was sorely inadequate to provide any guidance on this matter and, as a consequence, I veered off the road, wobbled across the gravel and ended up in a shallow ditch. With a stupid grin on my face, I relocated the road and gingerly pedalled away. Sooner than expected, the yellow glow of street lights penetrated the dark, wet evening as I approached Baddeck. The rain was strangely comforting as I turned down the main street to my accommodation.

The Green Highlander Lodge was quiet when I knocked on the door, but there was life in the Yellow Cello café situated on the street. Luckily for me, it was still open. I discovered that the both of them were linked and I was quickly shown to my room. By now it was about 9:30, so I enquired whether there was a bar nearby. I was informed that the yacht club, situated down a side street opposite the café, would be the place to go. I made my way down to the small harbour and on the left, overlooking Bras D'Or Lake, stood an imposing wooden building, which housed the club. I climbed the wide staircase and entered a large square room with a bar situated in the middle of it. I was told that I would have to make a donation towards the fee for the entertainment that night. I didn't have a clue of the going rate, so I gave five dollars, which seemed to be acceptable.

Now, music has been a huge part of my adult life, starting as a solo singer in the mid-'70s and then for three years as the lead singer in a local rock band called Blind Eye. During the '80s, I played guitar and sang with Brian as one half of a duo. All through the '90s and into the noughties, I was back as a solo artist and since 2007 back as the lead singer of the reformed Blind Eye. So, when the band struck up, I was more than happy to sit back, relax and listen to talented musicians giving their all.

The following morning, I decided to explore this small inland coastal community before setting out on the short 50km leg to my next stop. Baddeck is pretty village, built on a slight slope overlooking an inland sea. Many of the buildings are shingle clad and painted in lovely vivid colours. I walked slowly down the wide street and called in one of the ubiquitous souvenir shops to see what kind of gift to buy. I must admit that I was very disappointed with what I saw. I know it's all in the name, but I didn't expect to see so many Scottish souvenirs for sale. I hoped that Nova Scotia would celebrate more of the culture of its First Nation heritage than the heritage of a country 4,250km away. I posed this question a few days later and the reply was that it was a thing that the First Nations people in this area didn't do – what a shame.

I continued to the far side of the village and walked up a gradient overlooking the bay to a museum dedicated to Alexander Graham Bell, the famous Scottish-born inventor.

It displayed many artefacts donated by the Bell family and memorabilia associated with Bell's experiments. Apparently, in 1885, the Bell family stayed in Baddeck, and because this area reminded Bell so much of his beloved Scottish Highlands, he started building an estate for his summer home on a point across from Baddeck, overlooking the Bras D'Or Lake.

With my cultural box ticked, I was eager to set off to my next stop at the small community of Margaree Forks. To get there, I had to cycle back down the highway for 10km to a point at Red Barn Gift Shop & Restaurant, where I had to turn right onto the Cabot Trail proper. From there it was a leisurely 40km undulating ride, meandering through corridors of tree-lined beauty and passing through small rural communities.

My motel accommodation was situated on an elevated spot overlooking the road. It comprised of blocks of chalets joined together and had the feeling of an abandoned holiday resort. Disappointingly, it had no restaurant or bar, so I had to walk the short distance to the local supermarket to buy food and drink for the evening meal. I had been told earlier in the afternoon while having a late lunch, that I could get a drink at the local fire station situated outside of the community, but I didn't like the idea of drinking then cycling. So, I just lay on my bed watching the TV.

The next day would be a short distance of 37km to Chéticamp – a small fishing village on the west coast of Cape Breton. But first I had to find a place to have breakfast. Luckily, after only cycling 12km, I found the Duck Cove Inn, which was situated on the left above the road overlooking the wide Margaree River. I knew I had a good chance of eating there because there was a large sign on the side of the road stating breakfast was available from 07:30 till 11:00. My cleated shoes made a loud clicking noise as I climbed the wooden stairs up into the large empty restaurant (some people might say I sounded like a spaghetti Western hero on a bad day, but I beg to differ). Anyway, the friendly proprietor asked how I was and when I replied, "hungry", he told me that I had come to the right place. I read the extensive menu and chose the eggs Benedict. While waiting for my meal, I quietly gazed down upon the slow-moving river.

Suitably sated, I started the very comfortable 25km coastal journey to Chéticamp. It was a pleasure to peddle in the early afternoon warmth as the road meandered through large, long-established sand dunes. On entering Chéticamp, I found it well spread out along the coast, and at 4km, it's maybe too long to casually promenade along – if you ever felt the urge!

I soon located my guesthouse and, after checking in, I sought the nearest bar and spent a couple of hours relaxing and talking to the bar staff. Apparently, a large majority of the locals are Acadians and as a result many are native French speakers so it was good to hear them reverting back to speaking French whenever possible.

Walking the short distance from the bar back to my accommodation, it was obvious why the village had been established there. It is very well protected from the open sea of the Gulf of St Lawrence by Chéticamp Island situated a little way off shore.

That evening, I enjoyed a tasty meal back at the bar, preparing my body for the big push into the mountains the following day.

To continue cycling along the trail, I had to enter the Cape Breton Highlands National Park. So, the following morning I stopped at the nearby Chéticamp Visitor Centre to purchase a park pass. This I had to show at the kiosk situated at the entrance of the park before entering. From there, the smooth wide road started to rise slowly. Occasionally, it emerged from the blanket of trees, thus affording views of the stunning coastline below. After 12km, it swung inland, continuing on its upward trajectory until it levelled out after 16km. When I read of this recommended trail, it boasted that there was little heavy traffic to contend with, but all morning, large trucks had been belching out black exhaust fumes as they slowly wound their way up the mountain. Eventually, it became apparent why there was so much heavy vehicle activity. Large-scale road improvements were been carried out and therefore slow progress for several kilometres was endured by everyone. I was disappointed not to see any of the moose, which the numerous signs had told me to be very aware of, but with so much noise generated by the construction work, the moose had obviously sought quieter areas to frequent.

After 30km, I started the twisting descent down off the mountain. In front of me was the beautiful Pleasant Bay, a place visited by whale watchers from all over the world. On this scenic road, I met several cyclists huffing and puffing their way very slowly up to meet me. Many pleading, red faces looked at me for conformation that their ordeal was almost over and they were indeed close to the top of this strength-sapping ascent. To all of them, I wickedly shouted as I sped past, 'It's just around the next corner!'

After stopping for lunch at a quaint-looking wooden café in Pleasant Bay, I started along a wooded valley, which I hoped would cut through the mountain and deliver me, stress-free, on the other side. This proved to be true for the first 8km, but then, gradually, the gradient increased. Eventually and inevitably, I came to a standstill. My burning thighs could no longer propel me any further. The heat of the midday sun wasn't helping either as I pushed my heavy, laden bike up the road.

My only respite was the scant shade offered by small roadside rowan trees. Plumes of dust continued to rise around me as I slowly negotiated another section of road construction and my dwindling supply of water quickly became a concern for me.

I must have looked quite desperate as I slowly passed the queues of traffic waiting patiently for temporary construction lights to change, because two drivers gave me a bottle of water each from their cool boxes. Not once did I hear anyone shouting, as they sped past, 'It's just around the next corner!' A valuable lesson learned.

Red-faced and huffing and puffing, I eventually reached the top and my ordeal was over. Thankfully, I was rewarded with a wonderful twisting downhill section, marred only by the constant irritating squeal of my brakes reverberating across the wide, wooded valley.

Eventually, I reached the remote community of Cape North. It was there I knew I had to turn left and travel down another small valley to my accommodation. I had been notified by them that they didn't cook evening meals and therefore to stop at Cape North to either have a meal at Angie's family restaurant, or get provisions from the Cabot Trail Food Market. The blue and white painted single-storey family restaurant looked very attractive, especially when the large sign on the road stated "Fresh Lobster". So, I ordered two large lobster baguettes to take away and while they were being prepared, I popped down the road to the food market to buy three cans of ice-cold beer to wrap them in (this was the only way I could think of for keeping my baguettes cool…).

I quickly covered the 6km to the wonderfully preserved Four Mile Beach Inn. In this context, the word "inn" is a little misleading. It is not like a pub as we know in this country, but it is more like a guesthouse. In my case, my accommodation turned out to be a large, imposing, wooden 1880 General Store building. Immediately on entering, it was like stepping into the past. It seemed like modernity was still to arrive in the area. Contemporary artefacts were placed along the wooden counter with other items adorning the numerous shelves behind it. Looking very solid and taking pride of place in the centre of it all was an old-fashioned cash register. It was obvious that the present owners were keen to keep an authentic atmosphere and had spent a lot of time and effort creating a homely, nostalgic atmosphere. Their eye for detail even extended to other downstairs rooms, with most of the walls covered in old paintings and the solid brown furniture inviting everyone to sit down and rest. Even the exterior oozed character, with the walls and gables covered in white horizontal planking. A wooden fire escape snaked its way around and down the various sides, giving many vantage points to gaze down at the slender silver birch trees surrounding the store.

I was shown up to my spacious room and later in the evening, joined my host and other guests on the spacious back veranda. While consuming my lobster and beer, we discussed many topics, including the time when an American staying at the inn was reminded that the carrying of guns was against the law in Canada. It was a tense standoff before the host finally persuaded him to leave the gun secreted in his bedroom.

Breakfast the following morning was a strange affair. No one was allowed to access the tables on the back veranda until fiddle music was heard coming from a speaker hung in the hall. Luckily, this strange arrangement gave all the guests, like the start of a horse race, a chance to mingle, or recline in the number of comfy period chairs and make small talk in the various ground floor rooms. Nevertheless, there was an air of anticipation, because no one was sure as what to expect. But suddenly, Scottish fiddle music erupted from the speaker and the door out to the veranda flew open. Then there was this mad rush like musical chairs to find a seat before anyone else. When this chaotic dance had died down and everyone was seated, we consumed a lovely continental-style breakfast overlooking the beach just visible through the trees.

After checking out, I made my way back up the valley to Cape North. It was there that I noticed another guesthouse situated off the road. This would have been ideal, saving me the trouble of cycling 12 unnecessary kilometres. Yet, in hindsight, I was glad that I stayed at the quirky Four Mile Beach Inn, thus savouring its unique charm.

The 43km along the top of the mountain from Cape North to Ingonish started with a gradual climb interspersed with the now expected road maintenance before it gently wound its way down to the east coast at Neil's Harbour. From there, the road more or less hugged the rugged coastline all the way to Ingonish. Locating my accommodation was easy, because it was a very large colonial whitewashed wooden building, with a wide veranda all around it. I had a perfect view from my bedroom of the large freshwater lake beyond the main road.

Later, it was recommended that I walk the 0.5km down the road to a restaurant. There, I enjoyed a very good fish meal and drinks before returning and going to bed with my unwelcome, but half-expected, bedfellow called migraine.

Feeling refreshed the following morning, I set off with renewed vigour on the 93km last leg back to Baddeck. This meant taking the gradual climb up to the summit of Smokey Mountain in the Cape Smokey Provincial Park before the exhilarating descent and the return to the coast. The rest of my journey consisted of wide undulating coastal roads through small communities before eventually turning off the bypass back to Baddeck. I had booked a different guesthouse to stay in but still went to the yacht club for a drink and a lovely restaurant for my evening meal.

The following morning, I had to catch the return bus to Halifax, so I set off early to cycle the 14km back down the highway to Wagmatcook. Unsurprisingly, this return trip was quite relaxing. Gone was the anxiety of the previous trip. Even my young American friend was on board, so we exchanged tales of 13-degree gradients and stunning views.

The flight times back to the UK didn't allow me to fly that day, so I thought it would be good to finish my wonderful trip and spend one day in Halifax. So, I pre-booked a hotel in Dartmouth, which is located across the wide mouth of the Bedford Basin on the eastern shore of Halifax Harbour. Apparently, Dartmouth has been nicknamed the City of Lakes, after the large number of them located within its boundaries, but, I must admit, I didn't see any.

Luckily for me, the bus stopped in Dartmouth before crossing over the Angus L. Macdonald Bridge into Halifax. My sense of direction told me that if I got off at this stop, I should be close to my hotel and, sure enough, within 0.5km, the Coastal Inn quickly came into view. Later that afternoon, the young couple from Pedal and Sea Adventures came and picked up the bike and I was left to find a bar in which to have an evening meal and to relax in.

The following morning, I wanted to go into Halifax to see what it had to offer. I could have taken a taxi, or the bus, but because it was such a nice day, I thought I would walk the 3.5km to the ferry terminal and catch the ferry over to the lively Waterfront district. With its wide boardwalk wending its way around the various restored warehouses, seafood restaurants and cafés, it had a certain appeal. The sun was shining and there was a relaxed atmosphere as I casually walked around the main shopping area. The many bars looked very appealing and I'm sure you would automatically think that I would spend the rest of the afternoon in some of them before taking a taxi back to the airport. But, to tell you the truth, although I really enjoy going for a drink, I can't drink quantity. Three drinks are the limit before wanting to go to sleep. My room back at the hotel was not available and the sight of me sleeping on a park bench is not a vision I wanted for myself, so I just wandered around the city centre trying to get a sense of Nova Scotia's capital.

Late afternoon, I took the ferry back over to Dartmouth and retraced my steps back to the restaurant close to my hotel for an evening meal. I then returned to my hotel to pick up my one and only piece of hand luggage, which they had kindly kept safe in one of their offices, before taking the taxi to the airport.

The early morning approach to Heathrow was stunning, with a fantastic view of the Thames meandering through the centre of London. I was surprised that I could clearly see all the main landmarks and attractions that make the capital so famous.

It wasn't fair to ask Nia and Richie to drive all the way down to Heathrow to pick me up; instead I bought a train ticket from Euston. It was an easy transfer from the airport to the tube with contactless payment making the procurement of a ticket obsolete. I picked the first seat and settled down to an hour's journey into the city centre. I didn't think that I had jetlag, because I had slept on the return flight, but for some reason, I fell into a deep sleep and only woke an hour later when the carriage was completely full of standing people pushing and shoving for room. Luckily, I was wide awake when my stop at Russell Square approached and when I stood up, I discovered that I had been sitting in a priority seat all the way from Heathrow (no doubt, everyone thought I was a needy person).

After spending some time sitting on a park bench in Russell Square, watching people consume their lunches, I walked the short distance to Euston station.

Thoughts on the train

What a fantastic trip. The sun was shining most of the time. Accommodation was very good and the people friendly. I had no issues with the bike, other than the lights were poor. According to the other cyclists, the level of difficulty was moderate, but I found with the extra weight of the panniers, some of the sections were more than moderate for me.

Tales of whales in the waters just offshore, bald eagles soaring overhead and moose on the roadside proved disappointingly absent. The only sign of wildlife were the very dark blueberry-stained animal faeces littering the highway in the Highlands National Park. I'm sure that if it was not for the large amount of noisy highway maintenance, then maybe the wildlife would have been more willing to make an appearance.

I wish I could have experienced some of the First Nation people's heritage. I'm sure they have a plethora of traditions that people like me would find fascinating. There were indications on my maps showing that I had entered First Nation reservations, but with no retail outlet evident where you could peruse and possibly buy something, I was left disappointed. Maybe, if I had joined a supported group, then possibly I would have been taken to a place where they demonstrated their culture. But sometimes, if you are like me, unless you are wacked in the face by a large sign showing something, or physically stopped by someone, then certain things are not always that obvious.

If you feel the urge to go to Nova Scotia, then I thoroughly recommend you visit the beautiful Cape Breton and hopefully discover the Cabot Trail for yourself.

The Bear Essentials – 2018

Izmailovo Kremlin

After a rewarding trip around Cape Breton, I decided to cycle in Russia. I don't really know why I chose Russia. Maybe it was just a vain attempt to impress someone? Maybe it was just plain curiosity on my part. I know that Russia was never on the top of my list of holiday destinations. Unsurprisingly, growing up in the middle of the cold war, the Soviet Union was always seen as the enemy. The 45 years of tension between United States and the Soviet Union highlighted the genuine threat of a third world war and was always in the back of my mind. I think the whole world breathed a huge sigh of relief when, in 1991, the Soviet Union was dissolved, the Iron Curtain was lifted and the Cold War came to an end – a new Russia was born.

With this new birth, plus a reduction of tensions throughout the world, I was very excited with the prospect of visiting this new Russia. So, with this in mind, I tentatively searched the internet for information on the feasibility of this trip. I liked the idea of contacting a Russian-based company, hoping that they would look after me better. So, I contacted Vladimir Filippov from the Russian Cycle Touring Club (RCTC). Their website stated that they were established in 1996 and had extensive experience as organizers of Russian bicycle tours. So, after many emails, it was decided that I would join one of their supported tours from Moscow to St Petersburg. Although this might sound very exciting, what I really wanted to do – as I have always done – was to cycle solo. Unfortunately, that was not possible. As part of the Visa application, the authorities wanted to know exactly where I would be cycling and staying and certainly wouldn't allow the prospect of anyone cycling willy-nilly anywhere they wanted. Yet, thinking about it, my idea of cycling solo was absurd, given the size of Russia and me naively thinking that I would be able to secure accommodation easily, or a conveniently placed campsite would miraculously appear just at the right time. Nevertheless, I just hoped that I wouldn't be part of a genteel, silver-surfer-type group.

As the weeks passed, I was given the names of the rest of the group I would be cycling with. It consisted of Jacalyn, Jan, and George, who were Americans; Alan, a Canadian; Dag, a Norwegian; John and Jean from England, and me from Wales. I was given the option of sharing a room, but I didn't feel comfortable with sharing it with a complete stranger, so I chose to pay extra for a single room.

Alarmingly, as we started to finalise all the necessary arrangements, my excitement was immediately dampened with the headline news of the poisoning of Sergei and Yulia Skripal and the pointless death of Dawn Sturgess. After hearing that dreadful news, I questioned the necessity of the trip. I knew that Sue had voiced her concern, but selfishly, deep down, I hoped that the tension would soon blow over and everything would be back to normal. However, I did voice my fears in an email to Vladimir, asking him if I could delay the final payment to see if tensions between our two governments would ease. This, he graciously agreed to. Nevertheless, over the next few weeks it became apparent that Vladimir didn't think that it would make any difference to our trip and that I should commit to it fully. Although Sue was not keen, she recognised that I had gone too far to pull out and suggested I proceed.

As part of the Visa application, I had to fill in many pages of information to present to the Russian consulate. They wanted to know everything about me and my family, from the time and place of my father's death, to the passport details of my three daughters, plus the dates of any holidays I had been on in the last ten years. I thought the amount of information they wanted from me was ridiculous. But, eventually, I gathered all that was required.

To help with the visa process, the RCTC had emailed me all the details of the Moscow to St Petersburg trip. So, on a sunny Friday, and with half a tree's worth of documentation in a folder, both Sue and I made our way up to Manchester and the Russian Consulate. We found a suitable car park and paid for four hours, which we thought was more than sufficient, and made our way to the consulate building. There, we joined a group of people all applying for a visa.

Eventually, our turn came and I presented all my documents, confident that everything had been dealt with. Suddenly, the thickset man behind the desk declared that there was something wrong with the dates of my trip. I could have cried, but, true enough, the dates which the RCTC had emailed me were incorrect. He was apologetic, but could only suggest that I contact the RCTC and get a revised document emailed back to me. When I explained that, being in Manchester, I didn't have the means of contacting the RCTC, he did give me a ray of hope by suggesting that I come back in the afternoon.

After leaving the building, I did try at the Manchester library to access my emails, but that attempt was obviously blocked. Therefore, in the afternoon, and with a heavy heart, we returned and had to wait until everyone had been dealt with before again approaching his desk. I didn't relish the idea of returning home and then having to return the following Friday. Miraculously, though, he had the revised documents there. He had contacted the RCTC and they had emailed him the correct dates – I could have kissed him. The rest of the procedure went well, with him sealing all my documents and passport into a diplomatic envelope to be sent down to the Russian Embassy in London for processing. Luckily, we arrived back at the car park just before our parking ticket had run out, but it had been a close call. Two weeks later, my passport was returned with a Visa attached – I was on my way.

While arranging suitable flights to Russia, I noticed that it would be a tight schedule, with arrival times being very close to the early evening soirée in the hotel. So, Vladimir suggested that I arrive the day before, which would give me an extra day to explore Moscow. So, early on the 24th August, whilst holding onto my one and only piece of hand luggage, I flew from Manchester to arrive at 14:15 at Domodedovo International Airport.

I had been advised by Vladimir not to make my way to the hotel on my own, because I would be picked up by Valery. Now, I assumed that this Valery would be a man, but I wasn't sure and, as a consequence, didn't know who to look for. I hoped as soon as I entered the arrivals lounge I would see my name amongst the many pieces of card being held up high but, however hard I looked, my name just didn't appear. Three quarters of an hour is an awfully long time to walk up and down the lounge, scanning every little piece of paper in the hope of seeing my name. New drivers/escorts replaced the old ones as, like a magnet, they picked up their passengers. Eventually, I turned into the barrel chest of a huge man standing with my name on a piece of paper. He confirmed his name was Valery and apologised for being late. Apparently, the traffic, as in all cities, was very busy at this time.

We joined the slow-moving mass of traffic heading into the centre of Moscow. It was during this slow advance that we got on to the subject of the Salisbury poisoning. Valery was adamant that if you could not prove the Russian involvement, then you shouldn't accuse them. My reply was that I didn't have a clue as to the culprit, but after all was said and done, something did happen to two Russian subjects and one innocent British person had needlessly died as a result.

With this mutual stalemate sitting squarely between us, we arrived at the three-star Izmailovo Delta Hotel in the northeast side of the city centre. I have to admit that the view from the aeroplane as we approached Moscow was that of large concrete high-rise buildings dominating the city and I thought that this hotel would bear all the hallmarks of a bleak austere Soviet plan. Yet, much to my surprise, we stopped outside a bright modern hotel. Valery took me into reception and waited until all the paperwork had been processed before taking his leave.

I didn't know what to expect from a Russian hotel. I was relieved to see a large reception area full of glass-covered walls and people of all nationalities milling around. However, I was taken aback when trying to access the many lifts up to my room. A burly guard stopped me and asked to look at the correct documentation as issued by reception before allowing me to enter one of the lifts. After proving my right to be there, I made my way up to a spacious room full of all the mod cons associated with any modern hotel. After carefully throwing my one and only piece of hand luggage onto the bed, I returned and gave a courteous nod to the guard before exploring the hotel. On closer inspection, it emerged that there were two hotels joined together, both of them covered with impressive marble and glass walls, with wide staircases.

After finishing a cup of tea and a piece of cake in reception, my sixth sense kicked in. Before I knew it, I had miraculously found myself in the hotel bar and was very relieved to see the familiar sight of a Stella Artois pump on the bar counter. I'm not a lager fan, but gratefully took this amber nectar outside to a seating area. It was while I was taking in my new surroundings, a rather plain middle-aged woman on the next table tried to engage me in conversation. Trying not to be too discourteous, I looked at her and then back to my lager – my tall cool glass of lager easily won (now, before you start thinking what if she had been a young Russian beauty – the outcome would have been the same, because I am very happily married to Sue).

In the early evening, I walked the short distance to a grand-looking complex. It turned out to be the Izmailovo Kremlin, a wooden complex completed in 2007. This woodworker's dream was established as a cultural centre, celebrating traditional Russian architecture. As I walked up to this citadel, the vibrantly painted wooden onion-shaped domes reminded me of a Walt Disney-style fairy tale castle. Once inside this colourful and bustling complex, I could see several museums – one for Russian folk art, and, strangely, one to vodka. It is also home to the Church of St. Nicholas, named after the patron saint of crafts and trade, which, at 46m, turned out to be the tallest wooden church in the country. This brief visit whetted my appetite and I promised myself a longer look the next day.

The following morning I strolled through a lovely park adjacent to the hotel. It took me through beautiful groves of silver birch, along a tranquil lake and past large ornate buildings. On my return I explored the pedestrianised area around the hotel. Surprisingly, there was a Subway eatery and seeing as I was struggling to remember even one word in Russian, I called in and pointed to and then bought myself a baguette.

That afternoon, I returned to explore more of the Izmailovo Kremlin complex and, to my surprise, walked into an open-air market with open and covered stalls everywhere. At the back of the complex was what I can only describe as a two-storey wooden cloister with wide stairs accessing lower levels. From this high vantage point, you could look down at these crowded walkways and try to guess which items or produce they were selling. After negotiating several staircases, I eventually found myself amongst these ground floor stalls and was overwhelmed by the diverse range of goods being sold. You could purchase anything from books, baskets, retro toys, furniture, Soviet memorabilia, weapons, fur hats, nesting dolls, Russian artwork and, if you felt inclined, the complete range of Dremel rotary tool accessories. As you can imagine, I didn't buy anything; I just took a picture of a life-sized scratch built metal model of the superhero, Wolverine (as you do).

As I returned to the hotel, I walked past several familiar, if rather sad, bric-a-brac stalls, each selling unwanted gifts, worn and unfashionable clothing, worn-out electrical goods and the shoes of deceased relatives. Disappointingly, I didn't spot that (must-have) item from this array of uninspiring items, but you never know what could be lurking underneath a moth-eaten shawl!

By now, I was feeling nervous. It was close to the time when our group would meet in the reception area for the first time and I wasn't sure what to expect. Would I recognise them by the number of Zimmer frames they had, or by the dayglow pink of Lycra? I didn't even know what Vladimir looked like. When 5pm came, I walked into reception. I tried to look casual as I frantically studied the number of small groups in front of me. Thankfully, there wasn't a Zimmer frame to be seen.

I must have looked like the missing link they were waiting for, because a friendly American voice shouted, 'Well, hi there, you must be Gayreth!'

'Yes, Gareth,' I replied, emphasizing the "a" sound.

A slim, fit-looking middle-aged man came up to me and introduced himself as Vladimir and then introduced me to the rest of group. He then asked us all to join him outside in the seating area to discuss the various protocols and schedules. As a traditional welcome, we were given a pint of a dark Russian soft drink. To further strengthen my claim as the missing link, I spilt this concoction all down myself and had to return to my room to change my trousers. But they seemed to be impressed that I had at least two pairs of trousers.

After concluding all the paperwork, it was suggested by Vladimir that his son, Timothy, would take anyone who wanted to do some Moscow sightseeing. So, I joined the small group and walked the short distance to the metro station. Every metro station in Moscow can boast to be the most beautiful in the world. There are some stunning examples of richly decorated Russian architecture, which would grace any palace. Even the well-rubbed extremities of the bronze statues in Ploshchad

Revolyutsii station gave a sense of strength and pride every time you walked past them. Apparently, most of these beautiful stations were built up to the 1960s and they are a perfect example of Soviet art, with a lot of marble, grand statues, mosaics, stained glass, and chandeliers. Unfortunately, we didn't go to the more decorative ones, such as Mayakovskaya and Komsomolskaya stations.

After a little while, we emerged into the hustle and bustle of central Moscow, with the impressive neoclassical façade of the Bolshoi Theatre across the road from the station's exit. From there, we slowly walked alongside the crenelated wall of the fortified complex that is the Kremlin. We all wanted to see the world-famous Red Square and especially the St. Basil's Cathedral, which is undoubtedly the square's most famous building, and one of Russia's cultural icons. However, as we approached, it was evident that access was not possible due to a ticket-only concert in the square. We had to content ourselves with a brief glimpse of one the iconic steeples just visible from a side street.

By now it was getting dark as we crossed over the bridge looking at the adjacent Kremlin, glowing defiantly above the city lights. On returning to our hotel, I joined Alan and Jacalyn in the bar where we got to know each other better.

The following morning, a minibus came to transfer us the 260km to Staritsa and the 17th century Svyato-Uspensky Monastery. This white-painted complex is situated on the banks of the Volga River and was the starting point of our trip. For some reason, Vladimir wasn't going to accompany us as we made our way slowly out of Moscow and it was left for his son, Timothy, to guide us all the way to St Petersburg.

For 204km of this journey, it was on a smooth motorway, but as soon as we left it, the roads deteriorated rapidly. Luckily,

I was sitting near the front, because the speed and motion of the bus certainly wouldn't suit anyone who suffered from motion sickness.

Eventually, we turned off the road and down a slope to the Svyato-Uspensky Monastery. Our support vehicle hadn't turned up, so that gave us an ideal opportunity to explore inside the monastery complex. It's everything you would expect of Russian churches, with large frescos of saints and angels painted on every conceivable surface. Apparently, the complex had a chequered history with numerous changes throughout the years, from the burning down of the original monastery, to the building of new churches in the 21st century.

After marvelling at the workmanship on display, we went back outside and were introduced to Sergey, our support vehicle driver. I have to admit that I wasn't too impressed with the condition of our SAG (service and gear) van. It needed someone with good welding skills. The two back doors had to be opened and closed very carefully to prevent them falling off.

When I first contacted the RCTC, there had been an option to bring your own bike, but if I did, Vladimir couldn't guarantee that they would have the correct parts if something broke. So I paid extra to use one of theirs. Looking at the sad condition of the van, I was not too hopeful about the condition of their bikes, but, thankfully, all the bikes were well maintained and in very good condition. It took a little time for adjustments to be made to the bikes and to gain familiarity with the gearing, but as soon as our luggage was placed in the back of the van, Timothy loudly declared that we should all cycle back up the small incline to the main road.

At last, we were on our way, or least I thought we were, because immediately there was a shout from behind as one of the Americans, who was riding one of the two electric bikes, failed to peddle up the steep slope. My heart dropped. Would this be the norm from now on, waiting impatiently for other riders to catch up? Thankfully, this was the only time it happened.

After crossing the not-so-wide River Volga, we immediately turned right down a quieter side road and the start of the 55km ride to our first night's accommodation. After 5km, we turned right again, which took us across fairly poor, flat agricultural land. We were told to cycle at our own pace, with the proviso that if anyone held up the party too many times, or for too long, then they would have to ride in the SAG van.

Most of the time was spent dodging the potholes, which punctuated the road surface all too frequently for my liking. It seems that Russia will spend an obscene amount of money on the military budget, to the detriment of the country's infrastructures.

To break the monotony, we occasionally cycled past half-concealed hamlets made up of small wooden houses. Some of them were clearly occupied, while others looked like they were neglected weekend retreats, or maybe, more sadly, abandoned family homes no longer generating the lure or appeal they once had.

After 25km, we were pleased to see the SAG van parked on the roadside with tables laid out with food prepared by Sergey. I wasn't sure what to expect, but was more than happy with the tea and coffee, bread, cold meat, salads, fruit, and deserts on display.

Sadly, neither the scenery or road conditions improved after our stop, but continued to roughly escort us all the way to the turning to our accommodation. Sergey had conveniently stopped at the entrance to a long rutted lane, which led up from the road, across a wide open cultivated field and up to a large modern complex.

Arriving rather jolted at the hotel, I found it quite strange. There was a large, central, rectangular area with wide paviour-covered walkways on each side. Inside this rectangle were beautifully manicured lawns, which surrounded a large ornate circular fountain. The hotel buildings looking on to this central area were painted a vivid yellow colour, which contrasted well with the white uPVC windows and doors. So, you might think, what is so strange with that? Yet, it struck me that, for such a beautiful hotel and grounds, there should have been hundreds of people enjoying these facilities, with excited squeals of laughter coming from children and relaxed couples enjoying each other's company. Yet, for a complex of this size, it was virtually deserted. For some strange reason, it reminded me of a line in the song "Hotel California" – *"You can check out any time you want, but you can never leave…"* Maybe it was built solely for wealthy oligarchs, or visiting cyclists?

I was given a room at the back of the hotel, overlooking a not surprisingly deserted tennis court. Beyond its chain-link fence flowed the impressive Volga. It's stated that it is the longest river in Europe with all of its 3692km located within Russia itself.

True to form, I soon found the bar where some of the group were already enjoying a cool drink. This was an ideal time to get to know some my fellow cyclists better. Over the next few days, I discovered that George was a retired naval officer. Alan was a retired lawyer. John was a veteran rower and had worked in statistics and probability. Dag was a self-proclaimed vagabond, world traveller, consultant civil engineer on projects throughout Asia. Jacalyn was an editor, Jean, I think, had been a teacher and although Jan was friendly enough, she never divulged any of her private life to any of us. I also discovered that some of them had cycled with Vladimir the previous week and, as a consequence, were super fit.

With this diverse range of experiences, the international topics which were discussed when we all sat down to enjoy a tasty evening meal knew no bounds. Now, seeing my knowledge of international affairs was, at best, minimal, I wisely kept my head down and my mouth shut during those periods. Unsurprisingly, no one tried to get me to divulge the in-depth intricacies of carpentry and the correct sequences of hanging a door, so I just smiled and made small talk.

The following morning, after breakfast, we checked out and continued cycling on poor but quiet roads through rough open moorland and forestry. After 36km, we stopped at the museum of the famous Russian opera singer, Sergey Lemeshev. Now, you will have to excuse my ignorance of Russian opera singers; I had to Google him to get some information. Apparently, he was a well-known and loved Russian operatic tenor, active from the 1920s to the 1950s. Unfortunately, for me and my peers, if he wasn't on *Top of the Pops*, then he was completely off our musical radar. Nevertheless, the walk around his single-storey wooden house was interesting.

After lunch eaten on the grass verge outside the entrance to the museum, we continued to Torzhok, a fairly large town and famous for its unique architecture and gold embroidery. Our hotel was a large two-storey square building and my room was one corner of the first floor. I felt slightly awkward having such a large room to myself but, hey-ho, I had paid extra for it.

In the evening, we walked to a small restaurant where they specialised in making chicken cutlets called Pozharskie. At the entrance, we were greeted by two ladies, both dressed in traditional costumes. Then, when everyone was seated, they demonstrated the process of making these cutlets. I have to admit that I thought that it was delivered in a somewhat patronising manner, and although as part of the evening meal they were very tasty, I was relieved to step out into the cool evening air. After a guided tour of the town, we made our way back to the bar next door to the hotel just before the rain started.

The next day we had a bus transfer to Lake Seliger and the St. Nil Monastery, which was founded by Saint Nilus in 1594. The monastery is situated on a small island just off a small promontory. Strangely, we were not allowed to cross the bridge up to the impressive neoclassical yellow-painted structure until we wrapped ourselves in a sarong-style garment to cover our cycling shorts. I really don't understand why vivid cycling shorts and bare legs can be so offensive to a religion? Surely it's what's inside a person that counts, or am I being too naïve? Anyway, rant aside; we were given a guided tour of the buildings, with the restoration of a church being very interesting.

Before returning across the bridge, I visited a row of wooden huts which housed the medieval long-drop-style toilet. In this day and age, you would think that to mask the earthy smell emanating from below, there would be some sort of air freshener dispensing droplets of lemon, sandalwood, or even jasmine, but it seems that modernity was still to arrive at this monastery. Funnily enough, I didn't find this too distasteful, because it reminded me of a time when, as a young boy, the call of nature would sound loud and clear and I would have to scamper down the garden path to our own small solitary wooden structure. There, I would have to clamber up onto a twin-holed wooden seat and sit contemplating the baffling reason for having such shiny paper for me to use or, more often, until it was too cold to linger any longer.

Throughout the guided tour of the monastery, it had been raining quite hard, and we were cold and a little miserable, so it was decided that we wouldn't cycle from St. Nils, but continue riding in the bus. After a few kilometres, the rain stopped and those who wanted were given a choice to either cycle or continue in the bus. All but two decided to cycle.

It was while cycling along a wide, potholed road when a large 4x4 approached me at speed and then skidded to a halt in front of me before reversing quickly back up the road. He then stopped for a few seconds before driving towards me again. Apparently, Jacalyn, who was further up the road, while trying to weave her way around the countless potholes, had veered off the road and into the many small silver birch trees which lined the roadside. Fair play to the driver, who was driving fast, had seen Jacalyn career off the road, so he jammed his brakes on and reversed back to see if she was OK. This incident caused much hilarity because Alan, who had been following her, had been concentrating so hard on avoiding the potholes, he hadn't even witnessed the event. Later that evening, I was told never to buy a Russian vehicle. When the roads were this bad, most drivers fit extra strong springs and then travel at speed to negate the roughness of the road surface and ignore the damage caused to the rest of the vehicle.

Eventually, we arrived at our accommodation, which was situated on the banks of a lake. It consisted of two large log buildings. My first-floor room overlooked the wide expanse of the lake.

Seeing that this hotel was close to the water, it offered the chance to use an authentic Russian steam bath (banya). The small log cabin housing the banya was situated on the lake's edge and after we had all settled in, we made our way down to the banya and piled in. Most of us ignored a suggestion that we should all go naked in order to fully immerse ourselves in this unique experience and wisely wore our swimwear before sitting down in an ever-increasing cloud of steam. Now, if you were really brave, there were large pans you could fill with cold water from open-topped barrels and then pour over your head to invigorate yourself with the shock of ice-cold water. Also, if anyone felt the urge, there were small tree branches available for gentle self-flagellation.

My family will not be surprised when I state that I don't really like getting wet or cold and I was more than content with relaxing in the middle of this cloud of steam. This idyll all came to an abrupt end when Alan announced that he had gone outside and plunged into the icy lake. This was the last thing I needed, but seeing as I was the youngest one there, I wasn't going to let anyone know that I was a complete wimp, so I reluctantly followed Alan, who was going in for a second time. The small branches underneath my feet proved tricky to walk on and the sediment stirred up by Alan hid the sharper ones, so it was with great caution I tiptoed slowly into the lake.

I wanted to get this over and done with as soon as possible, but the level of the lake was only gradual and I had to walk out a considerable distance before the water had passed the giggle line and I was able to perform a shallow dive into the murky water. Trying not to use too many expletives as I surfaced, I turned around and made a far quicker exit than my entry and sought the sanctuary of the banya to warm up.

That evening, after dinner, there were intense discussions between three of the men about various reasons why there were conflicts around the world and the best way of resolving them and seeing as I had no experience of any conflict at all, I sensibly kept my thoughts to myself. While it had been very interesting listening to the different points of view being expressed, I had had enough by midnight and left them to it. Yet, so passionate were Timothy and John, they even continued outside their bedrooms, each trying to have the last say before retiring to bed. As I drifted off to sleep, all I could hear was John say, 'Yes I know, but...'

The following morning we were transferred along extremely potholed forestry roads. Eventually, we stopped at the Korpowo German War Cemetery and were told that we were to cycle the remaining 60km to the old provincial town of Staraya Russa. Before setting off, some of us went into the large field which contained 89 granite steles with 30,099 names of the German soldiers who had lost their lives during the Second World War. All war cemeteries throughout the world hold countless tales of bravery, self-sacrifice and needless conflict. These are mostly to appease their autocratic leaders and fan the lust for total domination, or maybe for some deep-rooted religious reason. Whatever senseless reason sparks off a war, in my simplistic view, I just think that life is far too short to continue killing each other.

After surviving a further 60km of Russian roads, we arrived in Staraya Russa, where one of the main attractions in the town is the museum of Fyodor Dostoevsky, the famous Russian novelist and philosopher. Again, I must show my ignorance of this man. I recognise the name, but to imply more than that, I would be lying. His home, nestling in the trees on the banks of the River Polist, is a large two-storey green-painted wooden building and still holds many of his writings and scribbling on display. The rest of the group spoke enthusiastically about his work, but, as usual, I just kept my mouth shut. From there, it was only a short ride to our hotel in the town centre.

For the remainder of the afternoon, we settled in and I went for a couple of drinks in the hotel bar. Later, we all got together for our evening meal.

The next morning, we had a short bus transfer to the small hamlet of Borki. From there we cycled a scenic road along Lake Ilmen towards the historic town and UNESCO-recognised Veliky Novgorod. On the outskirts we called in at the open-air museum of wooden architecture. This was of great interest to me. There were many large wooden buildings of various ages, e.g, village houses, workshops, chapels and churches. All of them were filled with contemporary artefacts such as tools, books, farm machinery, cooking utensils and sturdy-looking furniture. Some buildings had been newly erected, while others were being renovated. Outside some of the structures, artisans were selling various items made from wood. I could have stayed for longer, but we were on a strict time schedule, so we had to move on.

Veliky Novgorod is a very picturesque town with extensive wooded parks and well-kept gardens. Our hotel overlooked one of these expanses of gardens and my room had a full view of it.

In the evening, we had a guided tour around the town centre. The main attraction in the town is the red-bricked Kremlin (citadel) which is situated on the left bank of the Volkhov River. Within its walls stands a big bronze monument of historical figures built in 1862 and traditionally taken as a starting point to honour the start of Russian statehood. Also, there is the St. Sophia Cathedral, which is reputed to be one of the oldest cathedrals in Russia.

As we approached the cathedral, a large car and entourage slowly came to a halt alongside the 11th century building. I can only assume that he was the bishop, because everyone was on the point of genuflecting as he made his way up to and through the beautifully ornate front door.

We were told that if we were quiet, we could enter through a side door to witness the service. I think I may have mentioned this before, but I'm not a religious person and therefore I find it difficult to generate any feeling towards religious services. I can, however, appreciate how beautiful the interior decoration was and the intricacy of the architecture and I suppose there was a kind of atmosphere to the whole proceedings, but that was as far as it went. So, after five minutes, I quietly left and stood outside talking to our guide. When the rest of the group immerged, it was quite apparent that Jean had found this service a very moving experience and as a result was close to tears.

We slowly made our way back to our rather grand hotel. I was very impressed with the wide, white-marbled staircases which conveyed the residents to the four floors. On one floor there were glass cabinets which displayed an eclectic mix of artefacts which had been left by previous residents.

Later, in the bar, I was surprised to see that Guinness was available on tap. Pompously, I couldn't help but inform the barman that he was pouring this sacred drink far too quickly and he should let it settle before topping it up.

The next morning we were back on our bikes, gliding silently through the wooded park, watching children enjoy an outdoor funfair. Cycling over the River Volkhov, we made our way out of the town and along a busy road until we turned off. Most of the time, we were following the Volkhov through rural communities where the occasional dog would rush out aggressively, thoroughly testing our acceleration skills.

Eventually we arrived at the village of Selishchi and the end of our cycling. As we congratulated each other, we couldn't help but notice the red-brick remains of a large building. Apparently, it was the Arakcheev barracks. A military complex built between 1818 and 1825 by the Russian general and statesman, Count A.

A. Arakcheev. It must have been an impressive complex when it was first built, but now, it lies in complete ruins with precarious walls slowly succumbing to the inevitable advance of decay. Luckily, it just about afforded enough privacy required for male cyclists who wanted to relieve themselves after a long ride.

From this rather depressing place, we took the last bus transfer to the vibrant port city of St Petersburg. After negotiating our way through a maze of roads on the outskirts of the city, we arrived at our hotel. It was situated in a not too salubrious area, with what looked like a closed down hotel on the other side of the narrow street. Ubiquitous graffiti adorned its steel shutters and walls, all adding to the rundown feel of the place. Luckily, inside our hotel was fine and later in the evening we all sat down to our last meal together.

Throughout our trip, I had been compiling a poem about our experiences together and after the meal, I recited it to them. It goes as follows.

Why Do We Ride?

Why do we ride?
Is it to hide the stresses of life from perhaps a husband, or maybe a wife?
Or is it to feel wind through imaginary hair, to roll down a hill without even a care?
To sedately move at a leisurely pace, or head down, eyes out at the front of the race.
Is it to charge batteries in our everyday life, to charge up the body, or sometimes the bike?
Is it because, we spend too long at sea and need two wheels under us to make us feel free?
Maybe impress someone by ticking many a box, which may inspire that person to tick their very first box.

Now, is there a model for this riding we do, or is it just a random choice, just me and you?
But we know that we want it, it's always a good call – even if no one notices it when we take that first fall.
It's something inside we just cannot hide; it's a tug that's so strong that pulls us along.
We scan the horizon for a man with a van, with a plan to feed us and looking behind for someone to lead us, so we all can succeed.
Is it the reward at the end of the day, to shout loud and proud, I'm glad I experienced this day and reward ourselves with a glass or two, or sometimes just juice; that's a memory some of us will never lose.
We can't stop this conveyor belt from moving us on, but surely we can alter the speed.
By speeding up ourselves, we may slow it down, but with potholes and potholes around which we ride, the big ones have smaller ones lurking inside.
So, with care we can ride along happy, healthy in life's long, long peloton.
So why do we ride? Is there a need?
Dwi ddim yn gwybod. Diolch yn fawr iawn I chi gyd. (I do not know. Thank you all very much).

It seemed to go down OK and I hoped that everyone would recognise their own personal elements of the trip within the poem.

Timothy, our guide, had to return to Moscow after the evening meal, so he organised a female tour guide for the following day to show us the sights and sounds of the city.

The next morning, our tour guide took us to the metro station. As we descended, I couldn't help but notice the length of our descent. We were quickly told by our guide that

St Petersburg has the longest escalators in the world. Apparently, due to the difficulty of building escalators longer than 125m, the Admiralteyskaya station has two consecutive escalators. When it was built, it was decided to build one long 125m escalator to one level and then to build another, shorter, one at 25m leading to the station. I don't know if we were on that particular one, all I know was it took a long time to arrive at the metro.

St Petersburg is rightly called the cultural centre of Russia with magnificent bridges over numerous rivers and canals. Majestic palaces and cathedrals rise up from the cityscape. The very name is very symbolic: it was named in the honour of St. Peter, who is said to be the keeper of the keys to paradise. We walked the busy tourist trail and went into various shops and took many photographs of the highly impressive buildings. One included the shop front of Faberge, the famous jeweller of the Easter eggs.

These attractions were only a prelude, because our main focus was to visit the world-famous Hermitage Museum. To access it, we had walk through an imposing archway in the centre of the 580m long bow-shaped building of the General Staff. This opened up into the vast Palace Square, and beyond the massive Hermitage Museum stood proud. Set in five interconnected buildings, the Hermitage houses an impressive amount of masterpieces by artists such as Leonardo Da Vinci, Monet, Van Gogh, Matisse and Picasso, and it was a pure delight to study them up close. However, it was the Egyptian antiquities section to which I kept returning.

We were told by our guide that we could go our separate ways, so long as we met outside by the Alexander Column situated in the centre of the of Palace Square. Now, that was easier said than done, because when I finally dragged myself away from all these stunning exhibits, most of the square had been cordoned off for some military rehearsals and, as a consequence, the column was completely out of bounds. I didn't fancy jumping over the metal barriers and dogging the soldiers standing every two metres on the perimeter, so I just stood there as close to the column as I thought was sensible. After 30 minutes, I got bored, so I walked slowly around the perimeter hoping I would see a familiar face in the crowd, but no such luck. I made my way back to my original position and it was only after another 30 minutes when I saw George and Jan walking towards me. It turned out, that they were all waiting for me in a place just about as far as you could be from the column. When I explained to our guide, she apologised. This is one example of why I like to do things on my own.

Later, we all went to a lovely restaurant where a spare meal was put in a doggy bag. When we exited the metro on our return to the hotel a male beggar came up to us asking for money. I'm sure he was very disappointed when he was given the doggy bag instead.

The following morning, the rest of the group set off for a tour of the Peterhof Palace and gardens, but I was flying home. I arranged for a taxi to take me to the airport, where, in the departure lounge, I was questioned about whether I was taking out any Russian money. Even going through passport control, they wanted to know exactly what I had been doing and where I was flying to. All this information was readily available to them, but they just wanted me to confirm it. When my name was requested, I didn't think that they would have met too many Gareths, so I just hoped that this young gentleman liked football when I said, 'Gareth, as in Gareth Bale.' He just smiled and wished me a pleasant flight.

Thoughts on the plane

A little part of me was relieved as the plane took off. I had survived Russia, yet in all fairness there was never a time when I felt nervous or afraid. There were certain protocols to follow, but that's the same in any country. Everyone I met was very courteous and accommodating. My fears of being a member of an OAP outing were unfounded. Apart from the very first day, when I thought we would always have to wait for the older/unfit members of the group to catch up, we were always left to cycle at our own pace

We all have preconceived ideas of what a country is going to be like. Stupidly, I thought that modernity would be confined only to the major cities, but everywhere we stayed, you could be anywhere in Europe, with modern facilities at every turn.

OK, the surfaces on the quiet roads we travelled could be vastly improved, but let's face it, there are many country roads in the UK that need serious amount of work and money thrown at them to bring them up to anywhere near an acceptable standard.

It was refreshing to listen to my fellow cyclists, who seemed to have a far greater knowledge and understanding of the world around them than I did.

This was a very well organised cycle trip and I couldn't really fault it. Vladimir and his son, Timothy, spoke excellent English. The accommodation was good, with tasty food and we saw a variety of historic places.

I wish I could have seen the whole of Red Square not just a small part of a steeple.

Deep down, I still craved for the freedom of a solo traveller, but I knew that this was the only way to cycle in Russia, and I will remember it with fondness.

If you can stomach the interrogational style of assessing your suitability for a tourist visa, you will be rewarded with a memorable trip to a fascinating country.

'Oh yes, sir – most definitely' – 2019

Taj Mahal

Diverse, cultured, vibrant and incredible are just a few of the adjectives which have been used to describe India. Every programme I've seen filmed there shows a country full of stunning wild beauty, extreme landscapes, mixed together with layers of ancient cultures and history.

Although India has held a certainly fascination for me, there was always something in the back of my mind holding me back, keeping me just as an armchair admirer. The extreme heat and cleanliness was an obvious factor in my hesitation, but in reality, my most pressing concern was – would my constitution be strong enough to withstand the famous Delhi belly? Historically, this unwelcome accomplice has the potential to ruin any Indian trip and I questioned myself on many occasions whether I really wanted to test my strength in that regard. On hearing my dilemma, it seems that every man and their dog who has visited the country – and those who hadn't – tried to advise me on the precautions I had to take in order to have an enjoyable and safe trip. The talk of dire consequences that could befall me if I didn't follow their instructions to the very letter didn't bear thinking about. So, I had to be sensible and, I have to admit, I did question myself several times about the wisdom of making such a trip, but the lure of experiencing such a beautiful country swamped my initial fears.

Immediately after making my decision, I was struggling to decide which area to visit. One thing you have to accept is that India is big and being the seventh largest country by land area, you would have to choose carefully the areas that you want to visit. My favourite landscapes are mountains. So, after watching the ex-MP, Michael Portillo, on his railway journey up to Shimla, I knew that this former summer capital of the British Raj would be a part of my trip.

After much internet research, I discovered that I could take a train from New Delhi to Shimla, thus making the city an ideal starting point, so I decided to make India's capital my base to start exploring this vast country before continuing on to Shimla. I gathered information on the travel vaccines which I would need and over the next few weeks received the required jabs.

I reasoned that staying in a hotel in New Delhi for four days would allow me to acclimatise myself to the heat of an Indian summer and to slowly immerse myself into the unique ways of Indian life, while still holding on to my Western ideals and flushing toilets. I scanned the appropriate online booking agencies for suitable hotels and chose the City Star, which is a modern tourist hotel in the Paharganj district. It had good reviews and, as a bonus, was close to the New Delhi railway station.

As much as the four days in New Delhi was exciting, my main destination for my trip to India was Shimla. As I mentioned before, Michael Portillo rode on the narrow gauge railway from Kalka to Shimla. It looked fantastic, so it was a journey I wanted to recreate. Ideally I wanted to book return tickets for that leg of my trip. Unfortunately, I could only purchase a single ticket from Shimla back to Kalka. This posed a big problem of how I could get from Kalka to Shimla if not on the train? (I'll explain later). Frustratingly, I found it not that easy to book train tickets online. I went on to several sites before luckily purchasing a return ticket from New Delhi to Kalka. I was lucky that I was able to book and pay for three out of the four journeys before my card was blocked by my bank.

The day duly arrived and I was set to go. Everything (including a large pack of Imodium) was packed into my one and only piece of hand luggage. I felt confident that I had everything under control. I was full of excitement and anticipation as I flew out from Manchester Airport.

Now, one aspect I didn't know of about travelling to India was the restrictions regarding bringing Indian rupees into the country. Visitors, including tourists, are not permitted to bring any amount of Indian currency into the country. So I took a certain amount of sterling with me to exchange and hoped that my cards would cover the rest.

It was an uneventful flight and arrived at Indira Gandhi International Airport early on Friday morning. Luckily for me, the hotel offered a complimentary pickup service. So, after clearing passport control, I stepped out into the hot Indian morning. Immediately, I was confronted with a mass of white-clad taxi drivers, all trying to grab my attention, as well as my one and only piece of hand luggage. Luckily, one of them had my details, so I was confident that he was legitimate.

Driving away from the airport complex, I couldn't help but notice how beautifully clean and well-maintained the lawns and flower beds were. My confidence was growing, along with my excitement, as we joined the mass of vehicles heading for the city centre. As we approached the outskirts, the conditions of the road and surrounding areas started to deteriorate. Endless road works and long queues of traffic greeted us and the honking of car horns grew in intensity. To me, there seemed no way through this melee, and we surely would have to wait for hours, but my driver had different ideas and somehow managed to duck and dive his way through all of this chaos and emerged unscathed on the other side.

Looking out through the car window at the increasingly dirty streets, I couldn't help but remember reading a review, after I had booked my hotel, about the many beautiful places I could stay in New Delhi and places, like the Paharganj district, which I should avoid. It couldn't be that bad, could it?

As we drove through the city centre heading towards the Paharganj district, I tried to keep an open mind, trying to embrace this sensory overload, but when we turned down this one street, my heart sank. It looked like we had arrived at the local landfill site, with rubbish strewn all over the pavements, with unfinished building work propping up the shop fronts. I hoped that this was just a short cut to a nicer area and my hotel, but there, halfway down this street, in the middle of it all, was my hotel.

Stopping outside my hotel, I thought that I was doomed and the Delhi belly would surely pounce on me as soon as I left the taxi – licking its lips as it totally devoured me in one. All hopes for an exciting and exhilarating holiday vanished with my thoughts of being continually chained to a toilet seat.

Taking a not too deep of a breath, I gingerly opened the taxi door, half expecting to be immediately set upon by a latent belly. Then, quickly, like some criminal shielded from the press, I was ushered into my hotel.

Marvellous; what a relief. It was like stepping into another world, a world full of glass and marble, and a complete contrast to the chaotic world immediately outside. I was given welcome drinks and shown up to my room. Later, at reception, I changed some of my sterling into rupees. The hotel was everything that I had hoped for, with clean, modern facilities.

To celebrate this, I gathered up my restored confidence, and naively decided to fill the rest of the afternoon by going for a walk. Big mistake! As soon as I approached the front door, the doorman asked me where I wanted to go and stated that he would hail a taxi or tuk-tuk for me. I told him that I just wanted to go for a walk, but that only confused him. He informed me that no one goes for a walk, but I insisted that was what I wanted to do. I stepped outside and again was immediately confronted by taxi and tuk-tuk drivers all wanting to take me somewhere. I pushed through them and started picking my way up the street through all the rubbish left on the pavement. Now, I've worked in construction for most of my working life, so I'm no stranger to building materials left around, and I know when a job is only half-completed, but the work on these pavements had been abandoned. Half-finished work had been left to deteriorate and it was difficult to walk amongst it all without stumbling on discarded materials, or unlevelled surfaces. Where work had been completed, then those spaces were taken up by cars and scooters parked haphazardly along the pavement. In some cases they completely blocked the pavement and you had to step out into the road to continue further.

I continued threading my way up the street until a young man stopped me. He politely asked me where I lived. Was I married? What is the population of the UK? And finally, what was I doing? I told him I was going for a walk, to which he replied, 'Turn around and go back, there is nothing around here.' I took his advice and turned around and picked my way up past my hotel, past the New Delhi railway station and on to Connaught Place. There I was encouraged by a man outside a travel agent to go inside and receive a free map of the city. I was very wary of this offer, but felt I needed something to give me more information about the city. In hindsight, it was not the best decision I've ever made, because once I was inside, I was subjected to quite a barrage of questions about my travel plans and destinations. I informed them that I had all the tickets and paperwork needed for the duration of my holiday. Yet, they still insisted that those documents I had would be fraudulent and only their company could supply me with the correct documentation. But I held out and they eventually gave me my free map.

Connaught Place is one of the main financial, commercial and business centres and is of a circular construction with an inner, middle and the outer circle, with many roads radiating from it. It has chain stores, bars and Indian restaurants – very popular with tourists and business people and if you want to relax, the centre comprises of a large park, which is a popular venue for cultural events.

I decided to set aside exploring Connaught Place for the following day and walked the two kilometres back to the hotel and enquired about an evening meal. Unfortunately, the rooftop restaurant featured on the hotel webpage was being refurbished and therefore out of commission. Thankfully, one of the hotel managers came to my rescue and recommended a vegetarian restaurant with "hygiene of the highest quality", just up the street. I had no other choice but to take up his recommendation. So I gingerly made my way along the street and surprisingly made it safely to the restaurant. There, I was indeed greeted with a very high standard of cleanliness. So, after reading the menu, I tucked into a delicious dosa meal, which is a thin pancake or crepe, and because the restaurant was unlicensed, it was all washed down with a cup of tea. I was so relieved and impressed with the facilities, I ate there every night.

On my return to the hotel, I enquired to see if there was a bar close by, but was told that the only way of purchasing alcohol round there was to go to the opposite side of the street and buy bottles from an open-fronted off-licence. Now, this was easier said than done, because down the centre of the street was a continuous concrete barrier, about a metre high, which separated the flow of traffic. For some reason, there was no other method of crossing the street, unless you walked many hundreds of metres either up or down the street to a junction at each end. Fortunately for everyone, there were gaps in the barrier caused by large vehicles hitting it, although I'm not sure if the word "fortunately" is suitable. However, it did allow people to cross at those points. It looked absolutely suicidal to me and the thought of running the gauntlet by crossing two lanes of traffic and then clambering up onto this barrier, trying not to catch your clothing on the exposed metal reinforcing rods, and then negotiating the other two lanes, did not appeal to me in the slightest. Yet, the thought of trudging my way up to the junctions made me consider this alternative route.

I closely observed the method used by the locals, which was very simple. They just walked out in front of the traffic, assuming that it was the responsibility of the drivers to avoid them. I quickly realised that this was the way that Indian drivers drove around. They just react to what is happening in front of them. If someone suddenly stops, then the drivers travelling behind would just swerve around them. If that meant that they had to drive on the right, or up onto the pavement, then that was the appropriate manoeuvre they would take. The rest of the traffic behind them would then have to adjust accordingly. There was no courteously allowing each other to own their own space; it was every man for himself. If there was the smallest of gaps shown by someone who had momentarily let his guard down, then there was a free-for-all. Everyone would try to squeeze into it, whether it was a car, lorry, motorbike, pushbike, or tuk-tuk. A space was a space and it had to be filled, regardless of the danger which might arise from this macho style of driving.

By now the time had come and, with my heart in my mouth, I stood on the edge of the pavement, praying for a small gap in the flow of traffic. No such luck. So, I did the only gentlemanly thing I could think of, and that was to stick very close to an Indian woman, with the idea that she would be hit first and take the brunt of any collision. Miraculously, I made it up onto the barrier, but with no time to think of the consequences of the next step and like a reluctant wildebeest jumping into the crocodile-infested river, I was pushed from behind into the continuous flow of traffic. I nearly died of fright. How I managed to avoid a collision, I don't know, but survive I did.

I easily found the off-licence and pushed my way to the counter. I asked for two large bottles of cold beer, which were placed in a brown paper bag. With my two hands tightly grasping the beer, I made the daunting return journey across the highway of hell. It was only later in my room while drinking this well-earned beer that I realised that the price on the bottles was far less than the price I had been charged (lesson learned).

The following morning, breakfast was taken in the basement. It was only then that I realised that there were more Western tourists staying in the hotel. Up to that point I thought that I was the only guest staying there.

Now, in the grand scheme of things, Agra and the world-famous Taj Mahal isn't too far away from New Delhi, so I enquired at reception. They informed me that I could take a bus, train or private taxi. After ruminating over those choices, I chose the private taxi and booked a full day's trip for the following day.

I decided then, for the rest of the day, I would return to Connaught Place and explore it properly. Even after the now-expected battle of the taxi and tuk-tuk drivers outside the hotel and New Delhi railway station, the two-kilometre walk was pleasant enough. Even the sight of large dogs sleeping in the shade of the tree-lined road and the odd person recumbent on the pavement – obviously sleeping off the effect of alcohol or substance abuse – didn't worry me. More importantly, I promised myself to be more open-minded and accept that India is unique and has a lot to offer – if you allow it.

So, with this more tolerant attitude and my blue trilby straw hat and sunglasses firmly attached, I arrived at Connaught Place. It was at this point that my new tolerant attitude was sorely tested for the first time. The same man came rushing out of the travel agents, where the previous day I had been given a free map of the city. He declared in no uncertain terms that I was a bad man for not returning to book up with his company. I, in reply, told him that I had given no such promises and that he was in fact a bad man for shouting at me. I quickened my pace and sought refuge in the beautiful park in the centre of the complex.

It was while I was trying to relax in this inner area when I was approached by another gentleman who was more than eager to inform me that there were better places, like museums and galleries, and insisted on calling me an appropriate taxi that would take me there. I politely declined his offer, and had to quickly walk away like an Indian Runner duck to escape his eagerness. No doubt, his cousin owned the appropriate taxi.

All this helpfulness was starting to irritate me, so I decided to walk back to the hotel. Later that evening, I went to the restaurant and repeated my journey to the off licence before settling down to an evening watching the IPL cricket series on the TV.

I woke the following morning excited with the thought of taking the 223km journey to Agra. I chose the private taxi option because I wanted to be in full control of the day's schedule. So, promptly at 08:30, I was informed that my taxi was ready outside.

After weaving our way out of New Delhi, we were soon on the newly created Taj Express Highway. My driver was a cheerful young man and we were soon chatting about many things. He seemed a competent enough driver as we settled into our journey. But, as the morning progressed, I couldn't help but notice that he was more than willing to use his mobile phone whilst driving. I wanted to be reassured of the level of competency and qualifications needed to be an Indian taxi driver. He admitted that it was quite easy to obtain a driving licence by bribing an official, but insisted that he was fully qualified.

During our journey, though, I couldn't help but think about the many rules of the road, which all drivers should automatically adhere to. So I was a little worried to see the numerous signs lining the motorway reminding drivers to overtake on the right. Luckily for me, this motorway was a toll road and, as a consequence, it was very quiet. When we did eventually come up behind a large commercial vehicle in the middle lane, I was relieved to see my driver dutifully overtaking on the right. However, the next vehicle, he overtook on the left. I just kept everything crossed and hoped and prayed that there were no roundabouts to negotiate.

Now, I'm no saint, but I've never taken any illegal drugs in my life. Luckily for me, being brought up on a remote Welsh hill farm, the temptation was never there. So, I'm not au fait with the current drugs available, but I was very suspicious about the crystal-like substance that my driver occasionally put in his mouth. He explained that it was only a mild stimulant, which would keep him awake on this long journey. This really put my mind at ease! Thankfully, halfway through our journey, we stopped for a comfort break at a motorway station. It was while in the urinal, my suspicions were confirmed when I read a notice on the wall warning drivers not to take these types of stimulants while driving. I thought, *shall I have a word with him?* But thought better of it. It was a long way to walk back to my hotel!

The rest of the journey was uneventful and, as we made our way slowly through Agra, my attention was fully focused on the scene outside. The now familiar sight of vehicles slowly making their way through filthy potholed streets was now punctuated with carts being drawn by white bulls. Some of these large animals were waiting patiently until urged by their masters to push past these more modern modes of transport.

Reassuringly, the filth of Agra soon gave way to the filth leading to the Taj Mahal. I know that every country has problems with rubbish and litter, but you would think that if you had an UNESCO World Heritage Site, then you would surely try to make the surrounding area a bit cleaner for the countless number of people who visit every year?

As part of the booking fee, a guide was assigned to me. We met outside a hotel and took a tuk-tuk to the West Gate where I bought my ticket. After collecting it, I lined up to go through security. This consisted of two lines, one for Indian nationals and one for foreigners. The security line for Indian nationals was far longer than the line for foreigners.

Once inside, the 17-hectare complex – the "jewel of Muslim art in India" – revealed itself. The iconic view of the gardens leading up to the ivory-white marble mausoleum was keenly fought for. Fair play to my guide, he offered to take all the photographs needed to prove you had been there, even catching the refection of the building in my sunglasses. As we toured the immaculate gardens, he gave me all the history of Shah Jahan's grief after the death of his wife, Mumtaz Mahal, while giving birth to their 14th child.

You have to admit that it is a stunning building, with the main marble dome dominating the skyline. One detail that is not obvious to the naked eye is the four 40-metre minarets at each corner of the mausoleum were designed to fall away from the main building in the event of an earthquake.

I'm sure that most people would see this building as a symbol of love, but I was more interested in the actual construction of it. When my guide showed me the intricate lapidary inlay on the interior chamber, I was very impressed. He suggested that after the tour, he would take me to a small factory close by, where they made new inlays for the maintenance of the Taj Mahal. I should have known better. Although this factory did show me how they make the new inlays for the Taj Mahal, in reality, it was only a ploy to get me to buy some expensive souvenir. It took a lot of willpower on my part to stop them forcing me to buy something I didn't want. It was only after me insisting that I wanted to leave, did they relent and escort me to the door.

The return journey passed without incident, and as we approached New Delhi, I reflected on the day's events. I was very pleased to have seen this world-famous mausoleum. Despite a few awkward moments while in the factory, I thoroughly enjoyed myself. Also, I shouldn't have been too hard on my driver. At least he was awake enough to avoid a cow when it decided to take a stroll down the middle of the motorway. Safely dropped off outside my hotel, my immediate thought was food, beer and cricket.

After breakfast the following day, the doorman again asked me where I wanted to go. I told him that the Red Fort sounded interesting. He insisted that he hailed a tuk-tuk for me, because it would be too dangerous for me to walk. Now, it's quite nerve-racking travelling in a tuk-tuk. I felt too close and vulnerable to all the different types of vehicles trying to pass on both sides. Annoyingly, though, it was only after arriving outside its red sandstone walls that the tuk-tuk driver informed me that it was closed on Mondays. Obviously that little nugget of information was obviously unimportant to him or the doorman! It was a little disappointing, because I really wanted to see this historic fort, which served as the main residence of the Mughal emperors since the 17th century.

To compensate for my disappointment, and for a more than modest fee, my driver offered to show me the sights of the city. He started by dropping me off outside a rubbish-strewn street market. It was quite difficult to see where the rubbish ended and the goods on sale started. There was nothing I wanted or needed, so we quickly moved on. He then dropped me off outside Mahatma Gandhi's tomb, which is set in an immaculate garden. He told me it was free to go in and after passing through security, I approached the large circular enclosure. I climbed to the top of the mound and looked down at the open amphitheatre below. This is the place where, in 1948, Mahatma Gandhi was cremated and from the top I could see a simple but effective memorial to his honour. In the centre was a black marble platform with an eternal flame in the middle.

To get a closer view, I climbed down and entered a foyer. There, I had to take my shoes off, which were then placed on a shelf, before walking barefoot up to and around the tomb. On collecting my shoes, I was told that I had to pay a fee. I told them, in no uncertain terms, that when something is free, then it is free and walked away. I half expected security to stop me at the gate, but they didn't. I'm glad I went, because it was a quiet and peaceful place, but equally glad it was free. Apart from a well-manicured garden and a simple memorial, there wasn't anything else there to see. I'm sure that it has more significance to Indians who visit. They see him as a brave man who fought for independence in India and never gave up. Plus his belief in non-violence and peaceful protests to promote change is an inspiration to everyone.

We continued on to India Gate, an imposing Arc de Triomphe-style arch commemorating the Indian soldiers killed in the First World War. The area around this part of Delhi is wide open. It's quite impressive with the extremely wide road leading up Rashtrapati Bhavan – the president's official home. My driver then asked me if I wanted to see something cultural. Why not! So he took me to the Golden Temple. It's not the Golden Temple of Amritsar, but similar, with its stunning golden dome. After giving our shoes to another shoe-minding service, we washed our hands and feet, and donned the required orange head scarf before entering the temple. We were greeted by soulful music, all wrapped in a blanket of serenity.

One important element of these temples is that they provide free food to anyone who needs it. This is regardless of race or religion. I'm not into religion, but was humbled nevertheless by the idea of langar (community kitchen). To get a closer view of this gurdwara, I was taken into the kitchen to witness the preparation of the food. Huge metal cauldrons were sitting on noisy gas burners cooking the food while the Gursikhs who worked there, methodically stirred the contents. I tiptoed around on the slippery surface to where the people were sitting cross-legged in a large room. All were either waiting patiently to receive their food, or in the process of eating it. In another area I could see others, possibly volunteers, who were cleaning the empty tin plates, ready for the next sitting.

Leaving the temple, I couldn't help but admire the Sikhs when they devote so much to others. I try to help people if I can, but I know for a fact I haven't got the same level of dedication, or commitment, to do what they do.

As we drove back to the hotel, we were, as usual, caught up in large traffic jams. It was while we were stationary at a junction that a young beggar girl around the age of eight or nine, came to the tuk-tuk holding out her hands. I didn't know what to do. By giving her money, would that reduce her poverty? I didn't think so. The fact that she looked healthy made me think that she was most probably only the face for an unscrupulous gang close by. Nevertheless, it really made me question my response and my own feelings of *let's get out of here quick*. In hindsight, I wasn't proud of what I did, the way I ignored her, but surely it's up to each responsible country to alleviate their own poverty and not rely on tourists and other countries to fund the problem.

Sadly, my concerns quickly faded like the early evening light as we joined the mass of traffic and fans making their way noisily to the nearby stadium to watch the home cricket team, the Delhi Capitals, take on the Kings XI Punjab.

That afternoon showed me the reality of India. It's cultural juxtaposition between rich and poor, dirty and clean, wealth and poverty, chaos and tranquillity, all which are willing bedfellows, each tolerant of the another.

My time in New Delhi was fast coming to an end. Much to my relief, one of the managers confirmed that my own printed return rail tickets to Kalka were genuine. Also, he advised me not to listen to anyone who stated that they were not.

As I packed ready to leave, I looked out from my hotel window for the last time at the street below. I couldn't help thinking that if they blocked off the road for half a day and got a big lorry and slowly moved down each street collecting and cleaning as they went, then it would be a far more attractive area for tourists.

Anyway, any thoughts on New Delhi's public works department strategy soon vanished as I boarded the air-conditioned Shatabdi Express. The 268km journey to Kalka would hopefully take four hours, so I settled down opposite an English couple who were also travelling to Shimla. Luckily for them, they already had their tickets from Kalka to Shimla, but, as I mentioned before, I was unable to purchase such a ticket. I had read that I could stop at Chandigarh and then take a bus all the way to Shimla, or I could meet that bus from Chandigarh at Kalka, but there wasn't a guarantee that a seat would be available for me. So I decided to stay on the train all the way to Kalka and then decide which options were left open to me.

The journey was very pleasant, with food and drink handed out. I swapped stories with the English couple, who were very excited to have the chance of travelling on the famous narrow gauge railway up to this famous summer retreat. Another passenger who joined in the conversation was a Sikh lawyer from London. I think his name was something like Es Es and he was on his way to a wedding somewhere beyond Shimla. When he heard of my dilemma, he kindly suggested that I ride with him in the taxi that he had pre-booked. To say I was relieved would be an understatement, so I thanked him and offered to pay a proportion of the taxi fare.

After giving an Indian porter money for carrying my one and only piece of hand luggage the length of the platform (which, incidentally, he had snatched from me), we located our taxi and left Kalka.

From the station, the road immediately started to climb. We meandered our way through colourful villages with equally colourful people and the views just got better and better as we slowly made our way up into the foothills of the Himalayas. Several times we had to manoeuvre around large roadside constructions, which dramatically reduced the speed and subsequently increased the time taken to travel the 90km.

Halfway through our three-hour journey, we stopped outside a roadside shack. This brick-clad structure seemed to balance precariously on the side of the mountain. It turned out to be a type of café and Es Es and the driver were hungry. They asked me if I wanted something to eat, but I politely refused. It may have had "hygiene of the highest quality", but I wasn't taking any chances. While waiting for them, one thing I noticed, which seemed incongruous to me, was a sign on the wall of this isolated building halfway up a mountain boasting that it had 4G coverage.

Eventually, after passing through villages large and small, we arrived at Shimla, the capital and the largest city of the Indian state of Himachal Pradesh. I must thank Es Es for not just dumping me on the side of the street. They didn't have to, but he and the driver located a taxi rank (well, to be truthful, a taxi shack) so I could be taken straight to my accommodation. We said our goodbyes and I jumped into the new taxi.

I like maps. I find them easy to understand. I had a good idea where my accommodation was situated. So I couldn't understand why the taxi people were so baffled with its location. It was only after stopping on the side of the road that I realised I had made a mistake in not taking into consideration the elevation of Shimla. Roads on most maps are easy to follow, but here, most of the roads either wind themselves straight up or straight down. My accommodation wasn't just off the side of the road like it was suggested on the map, but was situated far below the road. Luckily for me, the taxi people contacted the B&B and a young lad was sent up to meet me.

We made our way along the narrow concrete road as it wound its way steeply down, passing various buildings and dwellings. A small path on the left then led us past a small school until it petered out in front of the guesthouse. The house was oddly-shaped because it had to conform to the small restricted shape of land it was perched on. I suppose it gave it a unique style and atmosphere.

After checking in, I was shown to my room, which had a fantastic view of the mountains. I had expected to see a circular green area close to the house, as indicated on my map but, in reality, it was the Annandale golf course and helipad, which from my bedroom window was about half of a kilometre below me.

From information on the internet, I knew that Shimla had a large flat area called the Ridge, where most of the iconic

Western-style buildings were situated. So I asked the proprietor the best way to get there. He stated that I should walk back up to the road and then cross over and start climbing the many hundreds of steps, which zigzag their way 800m up through a residential area to the Ridge. I decided I would do this the next morning. I then asked him about suitable restaurants, but he insisted that he cook an evening meal for me. He even instructed the young lad to go and buy some bottles of beer for me.

I'm not sure whether it was the high altitude or not, but a strange thought struck me while I was in my room tucking into the tasty evening meal. How does the sewerage system work on such a steep mountain? Because all I could see below my window were the roofs of houses seemingly built on top of each other, forever cascading down to the distant valley below. I certainly wouldn't feel safe living in a house at the bottom!

I felt content with my food, beer and cricket as the first day in Shimla drew to a close.

Now, Shimla has an average altitude of 2,206m, which I'm sure is the main reason I kept on waking up throughout that first night, gasping for breath. I've never been subjected to this kind of altitude before, so it was a little unsettling to say the least.

The next morning I had breakfast in my room and planned to explore the area. I also asked the proprietor about the bike tours which he advertised. He was a little vague, but promised to look into it. I told him that the only reason I chose his guesthouse was the fact that he advertised this activity. Anyway, I left that thought with him and started the long, slow ascent to the Ridge, which is a wide flat area, the *only* flat area and the epicentre of all tourist activities in Shimla.

Arriving breathless, I was greeted by a familiar view of shop-lined streets and small stalls. At the far end of the large open square was the imposing Christ Church with its dominant tower and light-coloured walls. To my left was the most stunning view towards the majestic, snow-capped Himalayas. Although it's called a city, it is small and, as a consequence, it didn't take me long to see most of its attractions. I'm sure that if I had Sue with me then it would have taken much longer.

If I have an hour or two spare in the afternoon, I tend to find a bar to relax in. I find going to different bars or pubs very enlightening. Usually, you can find a diverse range of people to watch. Red-faced tourists frantically scanning local information leaflets for the next overpriced excursion. Business people still on their laptops while eating their lunch and the retired brigade, meeting up to reminisce about the past and heartily boast about their newly acquired freedom – their previous work now just a distant memory. However, one side effect to having a drink in the afternoon is I feel tired and relish a quick nap. Usually, this is back in a guesthouse, B&B or hotel. But in Shimla, that would require me to take the long steep walk back down to my room. So, on this particular trip, I reluctantly decided to forgo this afternoon ritual. It was the same in the evening. I didn't fancy the idea of walking back up to the Ridge, having a few drinks and then trying to safely negotiate the hundreds of steps back down in the dark. So, each evening I defaulted to having food, beer and cricket in my room.

The next morning I again asked the proprietor about the cycling. He assured me that a guide would come and see me that evening at 17:30 to discuss the arrangements. Worryingly, though, by 20:30 he hadn't arrived and I was starting resign myself to the prospect of not cycling in India at all. However, by 20:45 a gentleman arrived and we arranged to start the cycling tour at 09:30 the following morning. Reading between the lines, I didn't think that the proprietor or this gentleman really knew anything about cycle tours. They certainly weren't imbued with a great sense of enthusiasm. I'm sure they were just mates doing each other a favour.

Surprisingly, the next morning he was there on time, together with a motorcycle crash helmet! Now, this immediately worried me. I had made it very clear the previous evening that it was a bicycle – with pedals – that I wanted! He noticed my concern and admitted that he was a biker, not a cyclist, but told me to look on the bright side, because a bicycle had been found for me. However, it had a small fault, which they were correcting "at this very moment". Well, we hung around for an hour, until it was suggested that we climbed on his motorbike and ride up to the road and wait for my bike there.

Eventually, at 11:30, my fairly modern mountain bike did turn up, with the nut securing the handlebars distorted and tightened to an inch of its life. Not waiting for me to comment on this hastily repaired work of art, my guide then suggested that he ride ahead and for me to follow. Apart from that brief statement, there was no further information as to where we were heading; he just disappeared into a cloud of black exhaust fumes, which belched from every vehicle moving nose to tail up the road. I shook my head and I took off after him. Fair play to him, he did stop at crucial stages along the route, waiting for me to catch up panting and gasping for breath.

After many hairpin corners, steep inclines, houses, shops and road works, we eventually arrived at our destination – the Shimla Water Catchment Wildlife Sanctuary. It was literally a breath of fresh air. I found it very cool and refreshing as I stood in the shade while my guide went into the sanctuary office to hire a bike for himself. It was while I was waiting for him that I couldn't help but notice construction work being done on the side of the office. A large concrete platform with reinforcing rods poking out at every angle was being built in preparation for the floor and walls to be installed. Like every building in Shimla, this extension was built on a very steep slope. Consequently, there was a huge drop to the trees on the lower side.

By now, even I was getting blasé about the unregulated face and nature of India. I was certainly not surprised to discover the complete lack of edge protection around the perimeter of this platform. But what I wasn't expecting was the sight of a young toddler walking around on this platform. It seemed that he was completely oblivious to the danger and certain death that awaited him only metres away. He was just content to play amongst the building materials and construction workers, and what beggars belief – the workers allowed it. If the HSE had been requested to research the occupational risks in India, then the agency would have a meltdown within the first ten seconds. Once again, I just shuddered and turned away.

With my handlebars retightened with an unsuitable spanner from my guide's toolbox, we cycled slowly into the forest. It was stunning. Bright sunlight shone through the canopy of mature trees and unfamiliar birdcalls accompanied us as we made our way along the forest track towards the abandoned water catchment reservoir. On our arrival, we were greeted to the sight of a concrete-walled reservoir, roughly the size of an Olympic-sized swimming pool. Originally, it was a gravity-fed harvesting plan, supplying fresh water to Shimla. After walking around the reservoir and looking down at the remnants of dark brown stagnant water, we drank sweet milky chai and ate biscuits given to us by a woman living in a very old dwelling close by (I didn't drink all of the chai, but did eat the biscuits).

On our return back down the forest track, we stopped at a flat, grassy area to have lunch. While relaxing amongst the trees, my guide told me that, as well as a biker, he was also a yoga teacher, and eagerly demonstrated various poses for me. Before I knew it, I was contorted into many shapes, which he promised was good for me.

Unsurprisingly, my guide said that he also had another company, which comprised of adventure-style activities and couldn't wait to show me the Facebook page on his phone. It looked very professional and I assumed successful. However, when I asked him how long he had been established and how many adventure-seeking people had used his company, he admitted that he had only started a few months ago, and, as yet, had no customers. He did, however, want me to post a "like" on his page, on the strength of those photographs. Am I being naïve here, or is it more important to have a large number of likes on your page than having a large number of fee-paying customers and good reviews? Anyway, I wished him luck with his new venture.

We made it back to the sanctuary office where thankfully an ambulance was not parked outside having to deal with the fall of a young toddler (no doubt, he will most probably live a long and healthy life). I gave my handle bar nut one more tweak and with a happy heart, took the road back down to Shimla and the B&B. It wasn't a long day's cycle ride, but at least I did some cycling. Even if the proprietor and my guide were ill-equipped to offer such a service, at least they said yes whilst crossing their fingers and I certainly saw a beautifully and peaceful part of Shimla.

My penultimate day saw me walking at a slower pace around the Ridge. During my few days in India, I found, to my cost, that if you walk slowly, or stop to look at something, then you will immediately become a target for someone to try and extract as much money as they can from you. To combat this, I adopted the habit of quickly scanning something or some place and then quickly moving on before anyone could pounce. But today, I tried to absorb more of what Shimla had to offer, so I walked slowly past various stalls, buying some small souvenirs before familiarising myself with the route to the train station. I knew roughly where the train station was situated, so I walked in that general direction. Sure enough, I spotted it down below me at a lower level.

To get there I had to continue walking along this road and find the slip road to the station. However, the road was very busy at this point, but, if you were brave, you could jump over the wall on to a metal gantry, which had been fixed to the outside of the wall. It didn't look particularly safe, just cantilevered, suspended over the now familiar steep drop. No doubt that this route, which every pedestrian used, was most probably far safer than walking on the road. Reluctantly, I'd come to except that in India, safety is not high on the to-do list. So, I just hopped over the wall just like the rest. Anyway, if it's good enough for the gentleman sleeping under one of the main metal brackets holding up the gantry, then who am I to worry, because most probably one of the many Indian Gods looking down would surely protect him and me!

My last morning in Shimla saw me walking to the station to start my 5.5-hour journey back down to Kalka. I was really glad that I had that ticket and was looking forward to travelling on this iconic narrow gauge railway and settled down to a memorable slow descent. All the carriages were full, mainly of Indian people and the sun was shining.

Although Shimla was, in Indian terms, less untidy than other areas, disappointingly, as we slowly pulled away, it quickly reverted back to the normal view of seeing discarded litter everywhere. It is said that on the top of Mount Everest, there is rubbish strewn everywhere. I know, at that altitude, it is impractical and verging on deadly to carry all your spent items back down with you, but what is the reason down here for not disposing of your rubbish responsibly? There was a young Indian family sitting opposite me and their two young kids were having a real good time, trying to see how far their empty crisp packets could fly up into the trees when they let them go. I know that young children don't really understand the consequences of doing something right or wrong, but surely parents should set the standards and show some responsibility regarding environmental issues.

My heart continued sinking as we made our way slowly down the mountain, pushing through what felt to me like a corridor of rubbish. I tried to block this demoralising view by concentrating on the beautiful vistas in the distance. From my seat they looked in pristine condition, but I knew that on closer inspection they would have the same amount of detritus smothering them. I nearly cried when I looked up through the trees and saw something like a slow moving avalanche of rubbish emanating from a small community above the track. I really don't understand it. How can a country so proud, elegant, and meticulously clean, have an attitude of "out of sight and definitely out of mind" when it comes to disposing of rubbish? Maybe, their infrastructure is not robust enough to cater for the disposal of rubbish – who knows? Encouragingly, there was one small glimmer of hope when we passed through a small town. A plastic-free enclave had been fenced off and a large sign boasting that this town was doing its bit for a plastic-free future, which proves that, with a little effort, things can change, even if it is only a token gesture.

This small iconic train eventually arrived in Kalka and I waited on the platform for a couple of hours for the next train back to New Delhi.

The return journey was pleasant enough, comfortably sitting in the air-conditioned compartment. Food and drink was supplied. I sat quietly observing the young, beautiful and enthusiastic students next to me planning their future together. Maybe they can take up the mantle of reducing India's litter problems?

It was dark as we arrived and I wasn't really looking forward to running the gauntlet between the station and my hotel. I thought I would be like a lamb to slaughter, but in all fairness, after pushing my way through the white mass of drivers at the station, the relatively short distance to my hotel was incident-free. My original room at the hotel was still available and, after checking in, I quickly fell into a deep sleep, ready for my departure in the morning.

Thoughts on the plane

It was a strange feeling, flying out of India. It is a fascinating country. Everywhere I looked I saw modern construction. There was extreme wealth, yet there was abject poverty. Colourful chaos merged with utter filth.

I can only comment on what I saw, but it seems to me the area surrounding my hotel showed a lot of informal or unorganised labour. I saw people working hard, but using lower technology-based methods. I hoped that they were trying to generate enough money to rise above their current situation. But, the sceptic in me doubts that the majority of those workers would change from working and creating something outside the constraints of legislation to join the rest of the world carrying the weight of H&S. I don't know, I could very well be wrong in my assumption, which is only based on a few days of observation.

I know, in hindsight, I wish I had been more adventurous, especially in my choice of food. I should have sampled the many different aspects of Indian cuisine. For example, every morning in Shimla, breakfast for me was only toast and jam. I'm sure the Indian equivalent would have been far tastier. In my defence, my hesitancy was fuelled by my fear for my delicate western stomach succumbing to the many forms of, real or otherwise, imagined bugs. Perhaps I was too cautious. For all I know, I could have been a long way from succumbing to these bugs, yet I could have been a *wafer-thin* amount away from total incapacitation and the ruin of a unique holiday. On refection, I think I got it right.

Regardless of what I think, she will rise every day, willing and enthusiastic, ready to say yes to everything thing you ask of her. What I do know is that she fascinates me. I would love to explore more of her uniqueness.

If you want to experience something different, then grab India with both hands and enjoy the ride.

The Craic – 2023

The River Liffey, Dublin

Since my last trip in 2019, the world has been a strange and often frightening place to live. The unexpected arrival of Covid at the beginning of 2020 gave us all a wakeup call. Early reports suggested that it was only a mild version of the Coronavirus' family, giving relatively mild symptoms with the likelihood of it blowing itself out relatively quickly. However, in March 2020, the World Health Organization declared Covid-19 a pandemic of frightening proportions. This intruder shattered most of our structured and predictable lives. Outside of war and famine, most of us had never experienced such frightening uncertainty. We stood in utter disbelief when we realised that our modern world could not contain such an indiscriminate virus invading our comfortable existence. The gravity of the situation soon became apparent with many deaths being recorded around the world. Reports of medical services being overwhelmed became a constant reminder of the severity of the situation. As the months passed by, we started to hang on desperately to the hope that the many scientists throughout the world would quickly develop an effective vaccine to combat it. Regardless of who you thought was the culprit and whether you thought that it was only a conspiracy, I for one am very glad of the sheer hard work shown by the countless and gifted, yet anonymous, people working behind the scenes to effectively contain this rampant invader. The dedication and commitment shown by key workers, put potential reservations aside to try and keep the world moving, to which I was immensely grateful.

As the months turned into years, and as a result of the sheer hard work of those nameless people, effective vaccines were produced and the world slowly started to tame this beast. With the relaxation of Covid restrictions, we all started slowly to return to some sort of normality. We know that Covid will not go away and, like the common cold, we will be bedfellows for the foreseeable future. Whether we gain some natural defence, or are protected through annual vaccination, remains to be seen. Those annoying restrictions have now been lifted and, as long as we show some common sense when required, we will just have to move on and live with it.

With this well-deserved freedom, I started to research countries to which I could cycle in. Initially, I had thought of Taiwan. Its majestic mountains and spectacular coastline would be an immediate attraction to anyone who wanted to visit it. But with the growing concerns of an invasion by China, I thought it would be irresponsible of me to put my family through unnecessary – real or imagined – worry. So I put that on the back-burner. My next thought was cycling down through the Baltic countries of Estonia, Latvia, and Lithuania. I have read that, despite being a part of the Soviet Union from 1940 to 1991, they all have a rich history worth exploring. I know that the Baltic countries are protected by NATO, but with the rise of a more aggressive Russia over the course of the last decade, plus the unfathomable invasion of Ukraine, I once again decided against it and put that on the back-burner as well. While these destinations were on my to-do list before Covid struck, I have to admit that my wild adventure streak has mellowed somewhat since I've retired. I sincerely hope that it can be rekindled, but in the meantime I thought it best to choose something not so demanding.

So, where do I go? The obvious choice would be somewhere near and where I haven't cycled before. We have been to the Republic of Ireland on several occasions, so why not explore the rich heritage of the Emerald Island on a bicycle and experience the world-famous craic.

Conscious of the fact that it had been three years since taking to the saddle in earnest, I didn't want to push the daily mileage too far, so opted to cycle roughly 50km a day and making it more of a sightseeing trip than anything else. Studying the map, a circular route around the midland regions with accommodation in the towns of Naas, Tullamore, Athlone, Mullingar, Navan and Dublin seemed to fit the bill. So, I booked a foot passenger return ticket from the port of Holyhead to the port of Dublin. I looked online and used the Just Park app to secure a week's parking in the Asda car park at Holyhead and booked suitable accommodation in those towns.

Getting up at 04:30 was certainly a wakeup call, but it was necessary to leave the house at 05:00 in order to cover 214km and arrive in Holyhead at 07:30. At that time in the morning, the traffic was light and I made it without any problems.

After cycling the short distance to the port, my bike was taken from me and secured somewhere in the hold. The crossing was smooth and I arrived at the port of Dublin at 12:15. After the usual hanging around at security, I cycled away from the port and headed for the city centre.

I had noted the roads I needed to take in order to navigate my way through the city, but stupidly, I didn't follow my own instructions and, as a consequence, got hopelessly lost. I enquired at a bus depot, confident that they would be able to put me right, but neither of the two drivers I asked knew the route I wanted. I even gave them the road numbers I needed, but to no avail. It seems that these road numbers were a complete mystery to them (I sincerely hope that they were able to find their way out of the depot in time for their next scheduled service!). In desperation, I retraced my steps and realised my mistake, eventually taking the correct road. Within a kilometre, I turned onto a designated cycle path alongside the canal and cycled away from the city.

It was delightful cycling in the warm weather because there were warnings of thunder storms in the area. After negotiating the many narrow country lanes, I made it to the outskirts of Naas.

Conscious of the fact that I hadn't eaten anything that day, I called into a small café and stood underneath a sign requesting everyone wait there until being shown to a vacant seat. After a minute, a waitress noticed my Lycra-clad body darkening the doorway. She inquired whether I was OK or not. I politely said that I was doing what the sign was instructing me to do and wait to be shown to a table. Her reply instantly reminded me of a young Mrs Doyle, the housekeeper of the two Roman Catholic priests from the very humorous sitcom, *Father Ted*. 'Oh bless you (Father) you have the patience of a saint.' I had this stupid grin on my face as I tucked into my sweet potato and roasted pepper soup.

Arriving at my accommodation on a residential estate, I was full of anticipation. The confirmation stated that I had to arrive at 17:00. Unfortunately, there was no one there when I arrived. I waited until 17:20 before asking one of the neighbours, but they couldn't help. I tried ringing the contact number, but seeing as I had a UK phone, that proved fruitless. At 17:35 I asked another neighbour and thankfully she gave me the correct dialling code. Frustratingly, there was still no answer. At 17:45 my phone rang with the host explaining that she had sent me an email earlier with the key code for the wall mounted key lock box. Now, this is all well and good if you pay for data on your phone, but seeing as I don't, I was never going to receive that email. No doubt this is a lesson that could be learned by both parties. After successfully entering the property, I had the whole house to myself to rattle around in.

I had no such worries in Tullamore, with the large modern hotel full of locals and visitors enjoying its tasty cuisine. The small room above a bar in Athlone was basic, but adequate. The large hotel on the main street in Mullingar proved misleading. It seems that the original hotel had purchased several buildings on either side of it, so now it has the facades of those previous properties, but behind them extends the huge expanse of the hotel. The private house on the outskirts of Navan was quirky, which gave you the feeling that you were in an antique shop, with the décor and every available surface taken up by furniture and ornaments from many different decades. My small room in a large townhouse in a quiet suburb of Dublin was comfortable. Over the week, I spent on average a €100 per night for my accommodation. However, the first three were bed only, while the last three included breakfast, which seemed strange to me.

Seeing that this trip would be a simple affair, I found that each day followed a predictable pattern. I would arrive at my destination early to mid-afternoon and, after checking in, I would find a suitable pub for some well-earned liquid refreshment before returning to my accommodation for an alcohol-induced snooze. Later in the evening I would go out for a meal and a couple of drinks. Most of the time, I cycled on quiet country roads and soaked in the beauty of Ireland. The nearest I came to any controversy was while I was cycling on a designated cycle path along a disused railway line and had to cycle through a thick cloud of very strong weed being smoked by a couple of lads seated precariously on a wooden bench.

As you would expect, the Irish are a friendly and charismatic bunch, quick to engage you in conversation and a delight to talk to, which reminds me of one certain gentleman not unlike Mr Michael D. Higgins, the Irish president, who approached me one evening while I was having a quiet drink. I knew from his demeanour that he wanted to talk, but seeing as I was studying the horse racing, I kept my gaze firmly fixed on the TV screen. Nevertheless, he still came up to me and said, 'You look like a ponderous man to me. It can be quite dangerous being a ponderous man. Where do you come from?'

I replied, 'Mid Wales.'

He looked up to the ceiling while stroking his chin and quietly murmured, 'Umm, Mid Wales'. He then turned to me and said, 'Well I'm just as bad, I come from Cork' then walked off.

As with all holidays, it was over all too soon. I leisurely cycled the 7km from my last accommodation to the port of Dublin. And despite the stormy weather, the crossing was fine. Thankfully my car was still where I had left it and I was back at home for 22:00.

Thoughts in the car

It was great being back on the bike, testing myself with self-navigation. Despite taking the wrong road to Dublin on my penultimate day and having to ask many people on how I could get to the city centre without being directed to the motorway, I had no real problems. I found the distance covered very comfortable and gave me confidence for the future. This first trip after lockdown was never going to be anything unusual.

As well as choosing it for its convenience and famously warm welcome I knew I'd receive, I wanted to see if I was still good enough to complete it. And as it turned out, it was just what the doctor ordered.

We all know that Ireland is a popular country to visit and this is borne out by the amount of foreign visitors I saw, (especially Americans).

So, if you want to savour the world-famous black holy water they call Guinness, or tuck into their seafood chowder, then make Ireland your next trip, you'll be like me – in heaven.

www.ingramcontent.com/pod-product-compliance
Lightning Source LLC
LaVergne TN
LVHW041248080426
835510LV00009B/645